MUSEUMS & GALLERIES COMMISSION

Acting Chairman
Lady Anglesey DBE

Members
Dr Frank Atkinson OBE
Dr Robert Begg CBE
Mr Lawrence Brandes CB
The Lord Dainton FRS
Mr F W Dunning OBE FGS FMA
Professor Sir John Hale FBA
Professor John Last CBE HON FMA
Sir Hugh Leggatt
The Lord O'Neill
The Rt Hon the Lord Rees QC
Mr R H Smith
Dame Margaret Weston DBE
Admiral Sir David Williams GCB DL

Director and Secretary
Mr Peter Longman

COMPOSITION OF THE WORKING PARTY
Professor John Last CBE, HON FMA, *Chairman*
Mrs Sandra Brown
Mr Brian Loughbrough FMA
Mr Neil Rees CBE
Mr Christopher Newbery FMA, *Secretary*
Ms Sue Bowers, *Assistant Secretary*
(until August 1990)
Miss Emmeline Leary, *Assistant Secretary*
(from September 1990)

MUSEUM & GALLERIES COMMISSION
16 Queen Anne's Gate, London SW1H 9AA

Contents

Museums & Galleries Commission

REPORT BY A WORKING PARTY ON LOCAL AUTHORITIES AND MUSEUMS

To:

The Right Honourable Timothy Renton MP,
Minister for the Arts

The Right Honourable Kenneth Clarke, QC, MP,
Secretary of State for Education

The Right Honourable Ian Lang MP,
Secretary of State for Scotland

The Right Honourable Michael Heseltine MP,
Secretary of State for the Environment

The Right Honourable Peter Brooke MP,
Secretary of State for Northern Ireland

The Right Honourable David Hunt, MBE, MP,
Secretary of State for Wales

On behalf of the Commission I have the honour to submit a Report by a Working Party on Local Authorities and Museums. The Working Party was chaired by Professor John Last, and its composition and terms of reference are set out in the Report.

Local authorities play a vital role in supporting museums throughout the United Kingdom. Those operated by local authorities represent a national asset of enormous educational and recreational potential. This report makes many recommendations, some of which will require additional expenditure. Others should help to save money and bring about greater co-operation. Professor Last's report is timely and I commend it to Ministers and to the Museums with which it deals.

LADY ANGLESEY
Acting Chairman

PETER LONGMAN
Secretary
1 February 1991

1

Foreword

by the Chairman of the Working Party

When we commenced our work on this report we had the ambition not only to analyse the current situation, but also to produce a report which would act as a basis for debate about the place of museums in our community. We were concerned to establish the present relationships which exist, and the purposes for which museums are created and subsequently maintained.

Our terms of reference were 'to consider the role and responsibilities of local authorities in relation to museums and galleries in the United Kingdom now and in the future, to instance ways in which local authorities may best provide support for museums and galleries and to make recommendations'. I hope that the report that we have produced will be regarded as wide ranging and authoritative. I believe that it has turned out to be much more of a 'think piece' than we had originally envisaged, but at this time of flux, particularly in the field of local government, this is probably no bad thing. I believe that our proposals though wide ranging, are practicable and constructive, and I hope that they commend themselves to the readers of this report.

I am very grateful to my colleagues, Sandra Brown, Brian Loughbrough, and Neil Rees who joined me on the Working Party, and to our Secretary, Chris Newbery, for his dedication and unflagging enthusiasm for our task. He has been most ably assisted firstly by Sue Bowers, and more lately by Emmeline Leary. Our thanks are also extended to Georgina Stagg for typing the report with care and patience.

The Working Party met eleven times and visited nine museums in England, Wales and Scotland to receive evidence. Some 140 written submission were received and a number of individuals and organisations were invited to give oral evidence. There was from the beginning, and throughout the period of the production of this report, widespread support from both local authorities and individual museums and galleries for the work upon which we were embarked. As part of the general consultation process, the Working Party presented its preliminary findings to the Museums Association Annual Conference in Glasgow in July, 1990 and more recently held a formal meeting with the representatives of the Local Authority Associations in November, 1990 to discuss a draft synopsis of the report.

Coincidental to our work, the Audit Commission has been compiling a report about local authorities and museums. We welcome the emergence of this report because, alongside our own, it cannot but be beneficial in informing the present debate.

Throughout the period of the inquiry, the question of the Community Charge and its possible impact on museums has been the subject of lively discussion within the museums community and beyond. The Working Party commissioned an independent survey into the ways in which local authority and independent museums were affected by the introduction of the community charge. Clearly, in England and Wales the community charge has only been in operation for one year and some of its implications for museums and galleries, both in the public and private sectors, are still uncertain. It is clear to us however, that whatever form of local authority financing is adopted for the future, it will be important that an adequate and reasonably assured level of resources is available to the museums sector if museums are to meet public and educational demand and to serve the community.

We are very grateful to all those who assisted us both in our visits and also in providing us with evidence. Within the obvious time constraints it was not possible for us to make exhaustive visits throughout the United Kingdom, but I do not think that this has detracted from our attention to the main issues.

Overall we have had a concern for the future wellbeing of museums that are supported by local authorities either directly or indirectly. I hope that this report will lead to a vigorous debate, some fresh thinking and an acceptance by local authorities as a whole that they have a responsibility for museums and galleries within their communities and to that end we hope that this report will help them formulate their policies.

JOHN LAST

Notes to the Reader

1. Throughout the report, the word *museum* is used to subsume *gallery*. The exceptions are either explicitly expressed or may be deduced from the context.

2. The term *Local Authority* embraces all tiers of local government in the United Kingdom. The exceptions are either explicitly expressed or may be deduced from the context.

3. The term *Registration* refers to the Museums & Galleries Commission *Registration Scheme for Museums in the United Kingdom*.

4. The names of organisations to which we refer frequently are given in full when first used in any one chapter; thereafter they are referred to by their initials.

1. Introduction

1.1   It is over 10 years since the Museums and Galleries Commission (MGC) published *Framework for a System for Museums* (1978) – the Drew Report – although separate reports on museums in Wales, Northern Ireland and Scotland have appeared in the intervening period. Since 1978, much has happened to affect the relationship between local authorities and museums. Notable changes have occurred as a result of the abolition of the Greater London Council, the Metropolitan County Councils and the Inner London Education Authority. While some museums simply transferred to other tiers of local authority, others became national institutions (National Museums on Merseyside) or independent organisations with charitable status (Geffrye and Horniman Museums). New challenges and opportunities have arisen for museums as a result of changes to the education system; in particular the introduction of a completely revised curriculum and fundamental alterations to the way in which schools are financed and managed. Then there is the community charge which, in its current form, is already having an impact on both local authority operated and supported museums. And there are the government imposed restrictions on local authority capital borrowing and revenue expenditure which create a difficult environment for museums, bearing in mind the fact that they are a discretionary service.

1.2   So far, we have concentrated on government initiatives which impact on museums. It is significant however, that many changes in the management of museums have been initiated by the museum profession. There has been a new understanding of the importance of setting and achieving standards in relation to all aspects of the museum operation, including the acquisition and disposal of collections, documentation, conservation, security, presentation and interpretation. This has manifested itself for example, in the introduction of the MGC's Registration of Museums Scheme which has been universally welcomed. Coupled with this emphasis on improving standards of collection care and interpretation in museums is a new realisation that the effective training of *all* personnel is absolutely essential. Within museums the traditional barriers between specialists are beginning to break down and teamwork, particularly in relation to specific projects, is emerging as a more normal feature of museum life. At the same time, there is a legitimate concern about the need to preserve scholarship, which should have its place in local authority and independent museums as well as in the National sector.

1.3 The challenges and opportunities that face museums are thus the result of both external and internal factors. In the report which follows we suggest many ways in which museums can provide a better public service by adopting suitable policies and practices. We also recommend that additional resources should be found to support museums. However, it would be complacent of us to assume that the case for investing in museums is self-evident. The Museums Association's definition of a museum (which has also been adopted by the MGC for its Registration Scheme) is a good starting point for understanding their value: 'A museum is an institution which collects, documents, preserves, exhibits and interprets material evidence and associated information for the public benefit'. It should be clear from this definition that museums are fundamentally educational in character. There are also important social and economic arguments for supporting museums.

1.4 Museums have always fulfilled an educational role in the widest possible sense, catering for visitors of all ages, cultures and tastes. In addition to providing informal education, the services made available to schools are particularly notable. The contribution to the formal educational structure has never been officially defined. However, its value has been acknowledged recently by the stipulation that schools should expand their involvement in museums in order to meet the revised educational requirements introduced by the National Curriculum. We discuss museums and education in more detail in Chapter 7.

1.5 While the educational role of museums is generally acknowledged there needs to be a better appreciation of the special contribution museums can make to the social fabric. At a time of rapid economic and social change affecting both urban and rural areas, museums can play a vital part in preserving and interpreting the heritage. They can give people a sense of place, local pride and identity. Museums can also be a positive force in promoting understanding of different cultures. Local authorities increasingly see themselves as having a major role in improving the quality of life, and museums have the potential to play a unique part in this process. We discuss the social impact of museums in more detail in Chapter 8.

1.6   Some local authorities recognise the way in which museums can boost the local economy. The Audit Commission in its recent report *The Road to Wigan Pier? – Managing Local Authority Museums and Art Galleries* (1991), points out that museums can help attract day trippers and tourists to an area as well as contributing to the marketing of a place and the attraction of new investment. The report cites the example of the Wigan Pier Heritage Centre which attracted half a million visitors in its first year of operation. Its success has attracted investment to the area and contributed to Wigan's economic regeneration. We discuss the economic importance of museums in more detail in Chapter 8.

1.7   Whatever the motivation behind a local authority's support for museums (and museums can be found in education, leisure and economic development departments within local government) it is important that there is a coherent policy framework for such support. After all, the overall level of investment is significant. Local authority net revenue expenditure on museums and galleries throughout the UK amounted to £92.8m in 1987–88 (see Appendix A) while local authority capital expenditure on museums and galleries in Great Britain amounted to £15.2m (see Appendix B). The number of visitors to local authority museums is also significant. The Audit Commission has noted that local authority museums in England and Wales attract some 20 million visitors annually – a figure which bears comparison with the number of visitors to the national museums.

2. Local Authorities and Museums: The Legal Framework

2.1   In England and Wales local authorities have been empowered to operate museums since the 1845 Act titled *An Act for Encouraging the Establishment of Museums in large Towns*. Under the *Public Libraries and Museums Act* (1964), local authorities have discretionary powers to provide and maintain museums or to transfer a museum or gallery and its collections to another local authority. The 1964 Act also included a number of specific provisions. First, it authorised admission charges provided the interests of students and children were taken into account and the museum or gallery was playing its full part in promoting education in its area. Second, it enabled local authorities to make grants towards the provision of a museum or gallery or advisory or other services related to them. Finally, it authorised the establishment of a cumulative purchase fund and permitted the proceeds of the sale of objects to be credited to this fund. Powers to use premises for educational or cultural events were given to both libraries and museums.

2.2   Under the *Local Government Act* (1972), museums in England and Wales became a concurrent function which could be exercised by both Counties and Districts. While Town, Parish and Community Councils are not specifically empowered to operate or support museums, a number do so under the general powers conferred by Section 137 of the 1972 Act. The Museum of London is established under the *Museum of London Act* (1965), as subsequently amended by the abolition of the Greater London Council, and various local Acts apply to local authority museums up and down the country.

2.3   In Scotland the legal framework for local authority museums dates from the *Public Libraries (Consolidation) Act* (1887), which gave local authorities the power to establish museums and galleries. *The Local Government (Scotland) Act* (1973), transferred this power to Regions, Islands and Districts. Less than ten years later, *the Local Government and Planning (Scotland) Act* (1982), restricted the power to Districts and Islands although Regions can make grants or loans towards expenses incurred by Districts or voluntary organisations. Under Section 14 of the *Local Government and Planning (Scotland) Act* (1982), a duty was imposed on these authorities to 'ensure that there is adequate provision for the inhabitants of their area for recreational, sporting, cultural and social activities', but it should be noted that museums and galleries are not mentioned specifically nor is there any attempt to define the word 'adequate' in this context. The *Education (Scotland) Act* (1980), allows admission fees to be charged by museums subject to certain conditions.

2.4 In Northern Ireland, District Councils are empowered to create and maintain museums by the *Museums (Northern Ireland) Order* (1981). We should note at this point that the local government structure in Northern Ireland is significantly different from the rest of Great Britain. Health and social services, education, housing, policing, roads, planning and other functions are all centralised, either directly in the Department of the Environment for Northern Ireland or through the area Health and Social Services and Education and Library Boards. Museums as such can only be supported by the Department of Education for Northern Ireland and District Councils.

2.5 There are some 800 local authority museums in the United Kingdom but the discretionary nature of the service creates an uneven spread of provision. In Northern Ireland there are 26 District Councils of which only 5 (19%) provide recognisable museums (see 4.19). In England and Wales, approximately 75% of local authorities incur expenditure on museums while in Scotland 70% of local authorities at Islands and District level run professionally staffed museum services, many of which also provide support in kind and/or cash to independent museums in their areas. A further 9% of Scottish local authorities provide substantial support to the independent sector where no in-house service exists, and all Regional councils assist public and independent sector museums in a variety of ways, in particular through their planning and education departments. The fact that the Scottish legislation requires local authorities to ensure adequate cultural provision in their areas has been a useful lever for the Scottish Museums Council in encouraging appropriate museum development throughout Scotland.

2.6 We have received evidence from museum professionals and professional organisations which criticises the existing statutory framework as unsatisfactory. The main problems are perceived as:

(i) The provision of museums is not a statutory function of local authorities.

(ii) Concurrent museum powers for Districts and Counties in England and Wales encourages overlapping provision and permits the existence of museums which are too weak to discharge their functions to a satisfactory degree.

(iii) There is no definition of a museum enshrined in legislation.

(iv) The legal status of local authority museum collections is not clear.

2.7 We hold the view that it would not be practicable to impose on all local authorities a mandatory duty to provide and maintain museums. However, we RECOMMEND that all local authorities with museum powers should adopt policies to ensure an appropriate level of museum provision in their areas and that these policies should be reviewed regularly. This does not mean necessarily that local authorities should provide museums themselves. There may be independent, university and national museums within a local authority's boundaries that would constitute an 'appropriate' level of provision. Furthermore, the nature of museum provision in adjacent local authorities may be a relevant factor.

2.8 Local authorities should be clear about why they are supporting museums before developing a museums policy. There may be many motivations relating to preservation of the cultural and natural heritage, the provision of an educational and recreational resource, the encouragement of economic development and tourism, and the promotion of social cohesion. Having defined its objectives a local authority needs to examine its own museum resources and those provided by universities, national museums and independent organisations in its area. It will then be able to develop a coherent policy towards museum provision, taking into account the other services it provides which relate to museums, such as planning, education and libraries.

2.9 We have referred to the need for a local authority to ensure an 'appropriate' level of museum provision. The Wright Report, *Provincial Museums and Galleries* (1973), defined the aims of a provincial museum service as follows:

(i) To collect, safeguard, and document evidence, material or otherwise, of culture, history and natural history with appropriate emphasis on its own area.

(ii) To make this evidence available to the public by appropriate means through, for example, the provision of suitable high quality exhibition space in strategic locations, and the development of museum education services.

(iii) To stimulate activities relating to these basic aims.

(iv) To employ and deploy curatorial, conservation and technical expertise appropriate to the scope of the collections and services.

2.10 The objectives of a local authority museum service as defined in the Wright Report are still relevant today. However, we have said that local authorities also need to look at museums provided by other sectors. Given this broader dimension we RECOMMEND that the following factors should be taken into account when a local authority assesses whether or not there is an appropriate level of provision in its area:

(i) The availability of museum collections relating to the historical, scientific and cultural heritage, and the natural environment of the area of benefit.

(ii) The existence of MGC Registered or Provisionally Registered museums within the area.

(iii) The public availability of museum resources throughout the year.

2.11 The MGC's Registration Scheme for Museums in the UK defines the nature of a museum and creates a policy framework for good practice when running a museum. The guidelines for the Scheme cover museum constitutions, finances, collection management, and public services. Minimum standards are laid down as appropriate. A particularly important requirement is the adoption of an acquisition and disposal policy. The collecting policy has to take account of other museums with similar collecting interests. We welcome the support of Local Authority Associations for Registration and RECOMMEND that all museums operated by local authorities should seek Registration. We also RECOMMEND that local authorities should consider Registration as a basic criterion when considering support for independent museums. We discuss the development of the Registration Scheme in more detail in Chapter 5.

2.12 Our recommendation (2.7) that all local authorities should develop policies towards museum provision would gain greater impetus with government backing. We RECOMMEND that the Office of Arts and Libraries and the Department of the Environment should issue a joint circular to local authorities after consultation with the Local Authority Associations. We also RECOMMEND that the relevant Government Departments in Scotland, Wales and Northern Ireland should follow suit. Their objective in promoting the idea of policy statements should be to encourage local authorities to take a strategic view of museum provision. In most areas there is considerable scope for local authorities to provide funding in such a way as to stimulate a greater co-ordination of effort among museums, for example, in the storage of museum collections. General advice on the formulation of policy statements can be obtained from the MGC and from Area Museum Councils which have considerable experience in promoting development policies.

2.13 We have already described the legislative framework for museums in England and Wales (2.1 and 2.2). Bearing in mind our recommendations concerning local authority museum policy and the implementation of the Registration Scheme, we consider that Counties and Districts should continue to have concurrent powers to operate museums. However, we RECOMMEND that the government should consider extending this power to Parish, Town and Community Councils in England and Wales. We would expect *all* local authority museums to meet the minimum standards laid down in the MGC's Registration Scheme, but this need not present a problem for the lower tier local authority. There are already a number of good examples of museums being operated or supported by Town and Community Councils including those at Trowbridge, Hertford and Pontypridd, each employing professional museum staff. A number of these councils have obtained delegated powers from District and County Councils and we welcome these links. At Pontypridd for example, the Town Council has recently acquired museum powers from the county and is running a full museum service with two professional staff and a revenue budget of £90,500 in 1990–91, better than some Welsh District Councils. It seems reasonable that explicit powers should be made available to Town Councils and their equivalents at the next appropriate opportunity.

2.14 The legislative framework for museums in Scotland was described at 2.3. We concur with the Scottish Museums Council's policy that local government museums and galleries should be vested solely in District (or Islands) authorities. However, we welcome the fact that Regional Councils in Scotland are continuing to support museums, and in the case of the Highland Regional Council we note that it has retained its directly funded museum service (the Highland Folk Museum at Kingussie) on the basis of Section 27 of the *Education (Scotland) Act* (1980), which gives Regional Councils a specific power to provide and maintain museums as part of their education functions.

2.15 We referred earlier (2.6) to a concern that the legal status of local authority museum collections is unclear. Advice on the legal position was included in the *Report of the Committee of Enquiry into the Sale of Works of Art by Public Bodies* (1964). It stated that 'the basic principle upon which the law rests is that when private persons give property for public purposes the Crown undertakes to see that it is devoted to the purposes intended by the donor and to no others. When a work of art is given to a museum or gallery for general exhibition, the public thereby acquires rights in the object concerned and these rights cannot be set aside. The authorities of the museum or art gallery are not the owners of such an object in the ordinary sense of the word: they are merely responsible, under the authority of the courts, for carrying out the intentions of the donor. They cannot sell the object unless authorised to do so by the courts ... because they have themselves nothing to sell'. This is, of course, only a legal opinion and so far as we are aware it has not been tested in the courts. However, the statement is important and welcome as a confirmation of a local authority's responsibility as a trustee for its museum collections.

2.16   It is our view that local authorities operating museums should be more aware of their trustee role. We RECOMMEND that there should be a strong presumption against the disposal of any items in a museum's collections as stated in the MGC's Registration Scheme guidelines and the Museums Association's *Code of Practice for Museum Authorities*. It is vital that this principle is accepted if people are not to be deterred from offering objects in future. There may however, be sound *curatorial* reasons for considering the disposal of items from a collection. In this situation, and where a museum is legally free to dispose of the items, they should be offered first by loan, exchange, gift or sale to registered museums before sale to other interested individuals or organisations is considered. Any monies resulting from a sale should be applied for the benefit of the museum collections, and normally for the purchase of exhibits for the collection. A more detailed account of the recommended disposal procedure can be found in the MGC's Registration guidelines.

2.17   If local authorities formally adopt the approach outlined in paragraph 2.16, it will be easier for curators of museums to develop a more dynamic approach to disposals in the interests of the collections. At present, curators are often reluctant to raise the question of disposal with local authority committees in case it leads to a more general policy which is motivated chiefly by financial considerations. The Audit Commission's report *The Road to Wigan Pier? – Managing Local Authority Museums and Art Galleries* (1991), suggests that clarification of legislation may be required in order to make the disposal of unwanted objects easier. We are not aware that curators are hampered in this way. What is required is a trusting relationship between the governing body and those responsible for collection management so that imaginative decisions can be taken without fear of setting awkward precedents.

3. Local Authority Museums

Diversity of Provision

3.1 Local authority museums have been described as the backbone of non-national museum provision in the United Kingdom. The size and quality of this provision varies considerably. Many of the largest provincial museums hold wide-ranging collections of national and international importance whose origins date back to the nineteenth century literary and philosophical societies and mechanics' institutes. These museums are to be found at District level and also form the basis of some County museums services. Examples of the former include museums and galleries at Bristol, Birmingham, Leeds and Manchester, while Norwich (Norfolk) is an example of the latter. In some parts of the UK, major city museums dominate the local authority museum scene. In the MGC's report *Museums in Scotland* (1986) – the Miles Report – it was noted that Glasgow, Aberdeen, Dundee and Edinburgh account for 75% of the total local authority expenditure on museums in Scotland. Furthermore, Glasgow spends more on museums than all the other local authorities in Scotland put together. These larger provincial museums tend to employ senior museum staff at chief officer level who report directly to a local authority committee.

3.2 The more typical pattern of District Council provision is for the museum to form part of a Leisure department; the senior museums officer is generally found at third or fourth tier within the departmental hierarchy and attends meetings of the committee only when museum policy or financial matters are being discussed. These District museums vary in size from smaller District museums services like Chichester in West Sussex to medium-size services such as Newport in Gwent. However, regardless of the size of the museums service, these District museums often hold collections of considerable importance. Taking the examples of Chichester and Newport, both museums possess excavated Roman material which is at least of regional significance.

3.3 We have already referred to the important collections held by some of the major County museums services in England. A characteristic of County museums services is the strategic role they have developed, particularly in terms of the assistance they give to smaller independent museums. A good example is the Wiltshire Library and Museum Service and its Museum Support Scheme (formerly the Pastoral Care Scheme) established in 1979. The scheme now incorporates 15 museums, including local authority owned museums, none of which employ a curator. Curatorial advice is provided by the County Museums Officer and two other staff. Conservators are also employed to advise museums and undertake treatment. Additional benefits involve the provision of storage materials and Museums Documentation Association record cards. All the services and materials are provided free of charge. Another example is the Lincolnshire County Museums Service and its development of a museum 'forum' which meets twice a year. The informal structure covers about 40 members representing many types of public and private collections. One of its successes, the publication of a leaflet listing museums in Lincolnshire has been of particular benefit to smaller museums. The leaflet, widely distributed in the county was subsidised by the County Council. Some District Councils also assist independent museums; the whole question of 'networking' is discussed in more detail in Chapter 4.

3.4 Local authority museums are sometimes compared unfavourably to independent museums. They are still regarded by a number of commentators as dull and dusty places, totally lacking in enterprise. This general characterisation is a travesty of the truth. The vast majority of local authority museums employ professionally trained and highly committed staff who have transformed the quality of service provision in recent years. Every month in the *Museums Journal* there are reports of major new displays being opened at local authority museums, and an examination of the list of Museum of the Year award recipients will show that local authorities are well represented. We commend museums services like Hull for devising new approaches to the presentation of local history ('The Story of Hull and its People', opened in 1990) and we welcome the fact that interactive exhibits are no longer confined to national museums and the private sector. Local authority museums have also been in the forefront of education initiatives and 'outreach' activities. We discuss these in more detail in subsequent Chapters.

3.5 While it is relatively easy to persuade a local authority Committee to spend money on new displays, it is harder to gain support for 'behind-the-scenes' activity. Large documentation and conservation backlogs exist in many museums, while storage conditions are sometimes deplorable. A particular concern is the lack of staff time, and sometimes expertise, available to carry out research on the collections. This research is by no means esoteric; it is essential to the proper documentation and understanding of the collections. We will discuss the need for greater investment in the care of collections in Chapter 6.

3.6 Many local authority museums play an important role as centres of expertise relating to the natural and man-made environment of the locality. In Leicestershire for example, since 1974 the County Museums Service has had statutory responsibility for advising the County Council and the nine District Councils on the geological, biological and archaeological implications of planning policies and development proposals. It has had similar responsibilities to national agencies since 1975 in the case of geological and biological conservation, and since 1979 (as the 'local archaeological body') to English Heritage. The total computer database of environmentally sensitive localities within the county now covers over 200,000 localities, many graded as to their importance, and the service assesses around 5,000 development proposals a year. Around 10% of the Department budget and 17% of the professional staffing is engaged on these responsibilities and functions of the service. Leicestershire's commitment is exceptional but is indicative of the way in which museums are not limited to caring for collections.

Structural considerations and the respective roles of management and committee members

3.7 There can be no standard blueprint for management structures within local government, given the differences of size and range of facilities. Museums may fall under any number of different local authority departments – leisure, arts, education, libraries, recreation, planning, economic development, environment, tourism, even central administration. The key to success is for museums to have a high profile within the local authority and access to the policy-making process. For a large museum the best option is for it to be a separate department so that the director is a member of the team of chief officers (see 3.14). A smaller museum can benefit from the support services of a conglomerate department provided that the senior museums officer reports directly to the head of department and has control of the museum budget, has access to a full committee and is properly involved in policy making and strategic planning. Evidence received by the working party suggests that senior museums officers at third or fourth tier level can experience difficulty in making the museum voice heard, especially if they are not members of the departmental management team. This is a particular problem considering that over half of local authority museums' directors are at or below fourth tier in the departmental hierarchy. As with most things, however, an enormous amount depends on the personality and political acumen of the museums officer concerned. This is far more important than internal or committee structures and points up the importance of management training for museum staff at appropriate stages in their careers. At the same time, it is important that senior managers or conglomerate departments have a good understanding of the museum function and of the role that museums can play in society. We welcome the trend whereby leisure and recreation managers for example, are receiving a wider and better training, thus encouraging them to look upon cultural and arts activities as equally important to those of sports and parks. The importance of a clear mission statement and forward plan for the museums service cannot be underestimated as a means of ensuring a proper status for the museum within the local authority structure. (see Chapter 5).

3.8   In the MGC report *Museums in Scotland* (1986), it was noted that some curators were being denied access to the local committee responsible for the museum function. This situation was by no means peculiar to Scotland but it is our strong impression that the implementation of the MGC's Registration Scheme is having a significant effect on such matters. The Registration guidelines state that an effective line of communication should exist between the senior museums officer and the relevant committee, and that the officer should normally attend committee meetings when museum policy or financial matters are being discussed. Happily the Registration guidelines have been endorsed by the Local Authority Associations and two years into the scheme no major problems relating to this matter have been encountered. We recognise, however, that formal access to committee can be a sterile exercise if this is the only contact. It should be but one component within a wider accountability by museum professional staff for their collections. The trustee obligations of local authority councillors to their collections demand that members receive the best advice and expertise to enable them to exercise their trusteeship properly, and this means both formal and informal mechanisms within authorities to ensure that such advice can be communicated between officers and members. Annual or more frequent inspections of museums and other local authority facilities by members have been a tradition in some authorities. These traditions are by no means anachronistic. Local authority committee members should also be aware of their role within the museum operation. We RECOMMEND that all local authorities should endorse the Museums Association's *Guidelines for Museum Committee Members* (1990), (see Appendix A).

3.9   Registration has also acted as a catalyst for local authorities considering the employment of professional staff to look after museum collections, and Area Museum Councils have been quick to point out the advantages. In London, for example, 11 of the 33 Boroughs have undergone significant museum development in the last 7 years. Seven have created totally new museums development officer or curator posts: Croydon, Hackney, Hammersmith and Fulham, Hillingdon, Islington, Richmond and Wandsworth. This is both encouraging and highly appropriate, bearing in mind that these authorities already held museum collections within library departments. We RECOMMEND that all local authority museums should employ professionally qualified and/or experienced curators in order that collections can be properly cared for and interpreted for the public benefit in line with the Registration guidelines. The alternative is to transfer such collections to the management of a registered museum.

Staff Conditions of Service

3.10   It has been a long-standing complaint by museum professionals that their remuneration is not commensurate with their responsibilities. We have received evidence that when job evaluation exercises are done, museum staff lose out in comparison with departments such as Technical Services and Treasurers whose tasks are deemed to be more essential to the functioning of the local authority. The point has also been made that the influence of market forces on salaries paid to professional staff militates against those professions such as museum staff which do not have private sector counterparts. There is a danger that this will lead to a two-tier status of professions within local authorities, leading in turn to problems of recruitment and retention. A further difficulty is that the salary of the senior museums officer may be depressed by the hierarchical relationship to the chief executive's salary which is subject to national guidelines and based on population levels in the area served.

3.11 Within the museums service as a whole there are marked variations in the rewards offered to people with equivalent responsibilities in different types of museum. The Reward Group's 1988 salary survey for the Museums Association confirmed for example, that staff in the national museums are generally better paid than their counterparts in local authority museums, although differentials at senior management level have narrowed in recent years. The result of these different pay levels is a general lack of interchange between staff in local authority and national museums, and this is regrettable from the point of view of creating wider and more attractive career horizons for people working, or wishing to work, in museums.

3.12 In the MGC report *Museum Professional Training and Career Structure* (1987) one of our principal conclusions was that the best hope for improved conditions of service is a coherent, accessible and well-executed training programme producing results of a quality which will persuade employers to pay more for quality of service. The work of the newly formed Museum Training Institute should assist this process. We have also received evidence which questions whether the present local authority conditions of service are best suited to the needs of museum staff and whether the availability of 'job-features' or 'fringe-benefits' might be beneficial both in recruiting and retaining staff. The benefits of training have been mentioned already, but clearly they can often be useful not only to employers, but are useful mechanisms to increase employees' job satisfaction. Paid sabbatical or research leave might be another avenue worth exploring, as might attachment opportunities to other museums of a different scale or nature, perhaps in the national or independent sectors. The Leicestershire Museum Staff Training Charter is a significant and commendable attempt to address these issues (see 5.31).

3.13 The diverse nomenclature attached to museum positions is another long-standing problem. The resulting confusion is unhelpful to employers, employees and the public they seek to serve. There is still a need for research to establish a job evaluation system which is capable of being applied in all types of museum. In the meantime, we suggest that local authorities should accept as evidence of good practice that those in charge of running a local authority museums service should be designated Director and enjoy the same status as that accorded directors in other roles such as schools and colleges. Evidence provided by one County museums officer went so far as to say that the lack of status arising from his position as head of the smallest section within a large department had hampered his attempt to raise funds from private sources. The title of Director would help to alleviate this problem, although we recognise that the structural organisation of some local authorities may make this course of action inappropriate.

Museums and separate departmental status

3.14   We have already made the point that a large museum should ideally form a separate department within a local authority. Birmingham is a good example of this situation, with its own chief officer reporting directly to the Leisure Services Committee. Separate departmental status for the museum has existed since the inception of the museums service in 1885, on the grounds of its contribution to the quality of life in the city and of the specialist management and professional skills required to execute its responsibilities for the care and presentation of the material heritage. Separate departmental status need not breed a spirit of isolationism. In 1989 Birmingham City Council set up a new Arts, Culture and Economy Sub-Committee which draws its members from the Finance, Leisure, Planning, and Economic Development Committees. Its central purpose is the creation and implementation of a cultural plan for the City drawing together all aspects of public and private sector arts and heritage activity within a single strategy to the mutual advantage of the cultural organisations and general public alike. It has already agreed policies for Heritage Development and Public Art.

3.15   Separate departmental status for museums need not be restricted solely to large local authorities such as Birmingham. Perth and Kinross District Council is a good example of a medium sized Scottish authority which at local government reorganisation in 1975, established the museums service as a separate department with the head of service directly accountable to the Chief Executive. However, local authority re-structuring exercises are steadily reducing the number of museums with their own chief officers running discrete departments. Brighton and Cheltenham for example, have both been reorganised in recent months with the result that the museum directors have lost their seats at the corporate management table and will be only second-tier officers. We trust that these changes will not diminish the role and position of the two museums. Together with the previously mentioned museums at Birmingham and Perth, they have achieved high standards of public service.

3.16 We understand the pressures on local authorities to streamline their organisational arrangements. However, we urge them to consider whether the additional administrative overheads involved in placing a museums service within a larger department (usually 'leisure') might be better applied to the service delivery end of the business. Furthermore, the impact of competitive tendering in the field of leisure provision needs to be taken into account. At Nottingham, for example, the Recreation Department has shrunk from over 800 staff to approximately 70. The Audit Commission rightly stresses the need for a strategic approach to service provision across the local authority's functions. The chief officer of a museums service can report to a leisure (or similar) committee in common with other heads of service; the committee itself thereby becomes the forum for co-ordinating activity. We therefore RECOMMEND that local authorities should regard separate departmental status for the museums service as the preferred option when considering their organisational arrangements.

Museums within larger departments

3.17 Having set out what we consider to be the preferred arrangements, we recognise that a number of museums services have flourished within the leisure environment. On the face of it the creation of a new Department of Leisure and Arts in Oxfordshire was detrimental to the museums service in so far as the status of the senior museums officer was reduced from Chief Officer to second tier. However, professional museum staff are well represented in the senior management levels of the Department, and the status of other professional staff within the museums and archives section has been enhanced by a re-structuring exercise. Two new senior managers have been appointed – a Head of Resources and a Head of Public Services – and the basic aim of the restructuring is to further the museums service's commitment to devolved management and clear lines of responsibility towards a truly integrated service. Budgets and management responsibilities are being devolved to 'heads of service units', in most cases curators of branch museums or managers of particular services such as conservation. The purpose is to focus attention at the 'service' end of the museums' activity and to ensure that decisions can be taken as close to the public as possible. This is completely in accord with the Audit Commission's recommendations concerning better financial management for local authorities.

3.18 The most exciting opportunities offered in Oxfordshire by the creation of the Department of Leisure and Arts are those of developing inter-professional projects linking the work of museums, archives, arts, libraries, countryside and other facilities within the local authority. A good example is the Reminiscence Project based in Woodstock which sets out to record the perception of change in the County through the experiences of local people. Project activities included oral history recording of memories; therapy in old people's homes with Social Services; drama presentation based on reminiscence; life story 'packs' prepared for residents of old people's homes; school projects recording grandparents; and the improvement of the library service to old people's homes. Through initiating and developing such projects the museums service has raised its profile in the Department of Leisure and Arts and is seen increasingly as a creative force. Projects of this sort receive all party political support and by carefully presenting reports on their budget implications the projects can be used as routes to improved funding, for example through enhancing exhibition budgets to present project results. In each case, plural funding is required, and that in itself encourages the local authority to provide support.

3.19 Kirklees Museums Service makes another instructive case study of the 'Leisure Services experience'; the complete account of which can be found in the 1989 Museum Professionals Group annual Study Weekend Conference Proceedings *New Times – Guide to Survival for Museums in the 1990s*. Kirklees Metropolitan Council was created in 1974 from eleven former local authorities, and their various museums were brought together with libraries under a Chief Librarian and Curator. For the next seven years the museums deteriorated in most important respects and visitor numbers actually fell. In 1981 libraries and museums were transferred to the Directorate of Leisure Services and a new Libraries Museums and Arts Division was formed with a Principal Officer (Museums & Galleries). An immediate change of philosophy was introduced. Museums were expected to increase their visitor numbers and make their facilities as well as their skills more easily accessible to the public. They were to join in the process of removing traditional barriers and participate in more general arts activities. Educational activities were to be introduced, while the buildings themselves were to be made more welcoming and comfortable to visitors. Museums had to collaborate with other sections of Leisure Services and other Council departments. If they had not done so and failed to deliver they would have been marginalised with potentially disastrous consequences. In actual fact, the museums have benefitted considerably during the 1980s, from a major capital programme including the refurbishment of most museum displays. This in turn has led to a significant increase in numbers of visitors. Oakwell Hall, for example, registered 10,000 to 14,000 visits each year between 1974 and 1981, but 88,000 in 1988–89 after a high quality renovation programme had been completed and new visitor services had been provided in the surrounding Country Park. It is also important to note that not all of the developments have been orientated towards visitor services. Many basic curatorial functions have been substantially improved or introduced, including the complete revision of documentation systems and the creation of a new central museums store.

3.20   The message from what has been achieved in Kirklees under leisure Services is fairly clear. Visitor services and educational work have undergone a radical improvement without being achieved at the expense of professional standards. Indeed the reverse is true. The willingness of the museums service to improve its own image and standards of visitor attractiveness and care has created a confidence in museums and their staff which has facilitated resources being made available for the care of collections where there had been precious little before. The importance of personal attitudes and relationships cannot be over-stated in this success story. This would be true whether the museums were in Leisure or under the wing of another large department.

Privatisation of museums: the Charitable Trust option

3.21   Compulsory competitive tendering has not been extended to museums as discrete local authority facilities. However, some local authorities may see advantages in 'privatising' their museum or gallery by transferring the operation to a charitable trust. We RECOMMEND that a local authority should only consider following the charitable trust route if it is doing so for positive reasons, such as the desire to take advantage of greater opportunities to raise money from private sources. Furthermore, a local authority should recognise that it will normally have to continue the revenue-funding of the museum's core activities on an indefinite basis if standards and service levels are to be sustained.

3.22 An instructive case study is Pallant House Gallery in Chichester, which was initially conceived as a local authority facility. However, not long after the Gallery opened, an agreement was drawn up between Chichester District Council and the Friends of Pallant House (1985) to create what amounts to an independent operation. The principal motivation for this change of direction was financial. The Gallery is now governed by a body of seven Trustees (four nominated by the District Council and three by the Friends) who appoint a management committee. The curator reports to the management committee but also has direct access to the Trustees. Financial support from the District Council covers the running costs with an allowance for inflation each year. As the costs have risen above the level of inflation, the Friends cover the difference, currently about 10% of the costs. District Council support will continue until March 1995, by which time the Gallery will be expected to have raised a capital sum sufficiently large (approximately £800, 000) to cover a good percentage of the costs. What happens after 1995 is open to conjecture although the close relationship with the District Council will presumably continue, bearing in mind that the Council still retains ownership of the gallery building and a substantial percentage of the collections.

3.23 Further examples of independent charitable trust museums devolved from local authorities are The Valley Inheritance, Pontypool, and the Black Country Museum, Dudley. A variation on this theme has occurred recently at Weymouth, where the Borough Council has made the museum collection over to a charitable trust, and in turn the trust's collections are being managed by Devenish Breweries which has established a visitor attraction called 'Timewalk' to tell the story of the town. All these examples of 'privatised' museums have special collections, themes, and locations which are attractive to tourists and can therefore rely on admission charges as an important source of income. Many local authority museums, however, hold collections of predominantly local interest and concentrate on providing community services. It is unlikely that privatisation will be appropriate for this type of museum. As one source of evidence put it: 'The issue of local authorities privatising the management of their museums is subsidiary to the objective of improving museums' ability to care for their collections and increase their use and enjoyment by the public. Unless local authorities are clear as to their obligations to their collections and specific as to their objectives in running a museums service, the exercise of hiving off their management will be irrelevant and unsuccessful. The clearer thinking now evident in some local authorities as to their overall role in relation to the community may, therefore, work to the advantage of museums who have identified their key functions and responsibilities and quantified the resources required to meet their objectives in a concise development plan.'

4. Local Authorities in Partnership

Joint Museum Committees

4.1   As we have already noted, Counties and Districts in England and Wales have concurrent powers to operate museums. In some cases they have joined forces to operate museums through joint committees, either on a regional or sub-regional basis. It is important to gain the full support of individual local authorities within a joint agreement, otherwise the museums service will tend to develop at the pace of the least willing partner. This was a difficulty for Beamish in its early years, and has certainly been a problem for the Tyne and Wear Museums Service. Some case studies will illustrate our theme.

4.2   The North of England Open Air Museum at Beamish was established in 1970 as a *regional* museum and is administered by a Joint Committee representing three North Eastern County and five District Councils. These local authorities make a contribution both to revenue and capital expenditure. The fact that Beamish receives two-thirds of its revenue budget from visitor income and raises substantial sums of money through a Development Trust means that it is often assumed to be an independent museum. Nonetheless, the commitment of the eight local authorities underpins the whole venture and they have been rewarded by Beamish becoming British Museum of the Year in 1986 and European Museum of the Year in 1987. This commitment however, is being tested by the impact of the community charge on local authorities in the north east. The majority of local authorities represented on the Joint Committee are cutting their revenue grant contribution by 50% in 1991–92, while capital contributions and credit approvals have also been significantly reduced.

4.3   Similar joint committees have been established to govern *county* museums services. After local government reorganisation in 1974, Norfolk County Council took over responsibility for the funding and operation of Norwich Castle Museum and its branches, together with museums in Great Yarmouth, Kings Lynn, Thetford and Cromer. The museums service is governed by a joint committee comprising elected representatives from both the

County and Districts in Norfolk, a County Councillor acting as Chairman and a District Councillor as Deputy Chairman. Decisions of the joint committee are reported to the County Council's Leisure Committee. Both museum buildings and museum collections (acquired prior to 1974) remain in the ownership of the District Councils represented on the joint committee, but all alterations or improvements to the fabric of the buildings required for museum purposes are borne by the County Council. Unless a District Council wishes to retain control of access to the museum building, for example for civic purposes outside normal museum hours, the cost of maintenance is borne by the County Council through the joint committee. All museum staff are on the County's payroll. The arrangements in Norfolk have worked well; economies of scale and the availability of specialist expertise have brought obvious benefits, while the local character of the constituent museums has been maintained. It would work even better if there was an improved overall level of funding for the service.

4.4   Hampshire County Museums Service is another example of a successful arrangement based on County/District joint committees. However, unlike Norfolk, there are three District level museums services which operate outside the County framework, namely Southampton, Portsmouth and Winchester. The County service consists of a central headquarters at Winchester comprising stores, design, conservation and administrative facilities, together with a number of small town branch museums scattered throughout the County. The branch museums consist of three elements: a permanent exhibition relating to the natural and local history of the area; a specialist display of part of the museums service's fine and decorative art collection; and a temporary exhibition gallery. Each curator of a branch museum has a specialist subject which carries responsibilities on a countywide basis. The branch museums are governed by a joint committee on which sit three elected members from the District and three elected members from the County. Revenue expenditure is shared between the County and District. If the building belongs to the District Council, the County Council will join in the cost of restoration; should the building belong to the County, it will undertake the restoration.

4.5   These arrangements have worked very well. The centralised system removes the need for storage space from the branch museums, thus providing more space for display. The curator's administrative load is reduced and access to specialist in-house services such as conservation and design is readily available. The provision of high-grade storage facilities at the Winchester headquarters allows good quality material to be acquired and maintained. The displays at the town museums have a strong local element and create a sense of ownership on the part of the community. This 'ownership' is bolstered by the existence of 'Friends' organisations at each of the museums. Pride in the Service at both County and District level has led to investment in the museums, and staff morale appears to have benefitted. In short, this is an exemplary model which might well be translated to other parts of England and Wales.

4.6 The arguments in favour of an integrated County service were employed when the future of the Tyne and Wear Museums Service was uncertain as a result of the abolition of the Tyne and Wear Metropolitan County Council in 1986. It was subsequently agreed that the Tyne and Wear Museums Service should be retained as a county-wide service, and it was placed under the control of a joint museums committee comprising the five successor District authorities in Tyne and Wear. A financial contribution from central government (via the MGC) towards the revenue costs of the museums service is provided on the basis that the local authorities continue to maintain a unitary service. The joint agreement drawn up in 1986 has proved to be inflexible and new financial arrangements are being introduced with a view to dealing with the different aspirations of individual Districts. From 1991–92, each District will be charged for the cost of providing the museums service in its area. This charge will consist of the actual costs related to the local museum buildings; 'standard' costs related to staffing and associated items as agreed with individual Districts; and costs relating to conservation, security, and research and development based on the joint museums service assessment of the needs of the collection in each area. Thus, one District will be able to vary elements of the service level within its area, for example, opening hours and the numbers and type of exhibitions, without affecting the financial contributions of other Districts. Central administration costs will be a first charge on the government grant. Nevertheless, these arrangements will rely on the willingness and the ability of individual Districts to work together and to provide realistic financial contributions.

4.7 In Scotland, we have already noted that museum powers are limited to Districts, but it is permissible for a number of them to provide a museums service on a joint basis. So far there is only one established example in Scotland; the North East Scotland Museums

Service (NESMS). This Service is governed by a joint committee formed of elected representatives from the three Districts of Banff and Buchan, Gordon and Kincardine and Deeside, and it consists of six museums together with workshops and storage facilities. Similar joint museums services might be appropriate in other parts of Scotland but, as we have already said, success depends on commitment from all those involved. It was noted in the Miles Report that 'the combined expenditure in the NESMS appears to be well below what is required for a local authority service covering such a large area'. It is no good entering into a partnership if economy is the only motivation – a high quality of service provision is equally important.

Museum Networking

4.8 The idea of museum networking is not new, and local authorities have generally played their part in creating and sustaining museum organisations whose objectives are to share information and expertise and to provide services and facilities for the common good. Thus, in varying degrees, networking includes such organisations as Regional Museums Federations, Area Museum Councils (AMCs) and Countywide Consultative Committees.

4.9 In the MGC's *Review of Area Museum Councils and services* (1984) an AMC was defined as 'a membership organisation consisting of representatives of museums and the organisations which run them, with the objective of helping local museums to improve the standards of care for their collections and service to the public. This is done by fostering and increasing co-operation, providing common services and information, and distributing government grants to approved projects'. The report noted that AMCs originated from those local authorities which ran museums. While their membership has since reduced as a proportion of the total (largely due to the rise in the number of independent museums seeking membership), the influence of local authorities still predominates and they account for a far higher percentage of the total expenditure on museums. The continued involvement of local authorities in the affairs of AMCs is mutually beneficial. On the one hand, AMCs benefit from subscriptions and donations provided by local authorities while, on the other, local authority museums are eligible for a wide range of services and grants. The latter can assist virtually any aspect of a museum's operation with the exception of routine running costs, purchase of exhibits, and (in England) capital developments involving building work. However, local authority involvement is also vital at a strategic level, assisting AMCs in their efforts to promote museum co-operation and development on a regional and sub-regional basis. We RECOMMEND that all local authorities with museum responsibilities should become members of AMCs. There is no doubt that the work of the AMCs over the last 30 years has contributed to a vast improvement in museum standards, particularly in respect of caring for collections. AMCs have also been agents of change in promoting the idea that museums should produce development or business plans, and there has been a new emphasis on training museum personnel and raising consciousness about marketing. The need for additional resources so that AMCs can continue to be effective in their work is highlighted in Chapter 6.

4.10 Complementary to the work of the AMCs is the activity of Countywide Consultative Committees (CCCs), or Forums as they tend to be known in the north of England and Scotland. The MGC report *Countywide Consultative Committees for Museums* (1982) rehearsed the view that the chief cause of weakness in the museum world in the United Kingdom is its fragmentation. It argued that, despite re-organisation of local government in 1974, the concept of the 'county' was still of use as a central basis for museum activities. The role of CCCs was defined as follows:

(i) To ensure that all museum needs within a county area are properly and adequately covered.

(ii) To ensure that sufficient resources are made available to those museums within the county which are either weak or removed from the large centres of population.

(iii) To avoid duplication of effort, by rationalising collecting policies, encouraging the sharing of staff, or otherwise.

(iv) To encourage co-operation among museums of different kinds, for example, local authority and service museums.

(v) To promote the setting up of adequate recording facilities (eg. biological, archaeological, historical, industrial) within the county.

(vi) To generate and encourage new ideas (eg. in interpretation) in an unhurried way and with the long term view, suggesting where pilot schemes might be established with countywide financial and professional support.

(vii) To advise AMCs on priorities in the distribution of resources.

4.11   It was recommended that representation on a CCC should be wide as practicable. Particular importance was attached to the involvement of local authority elected members (as distinct from curators) because it was recognised that this would be the best means of convincing local authorities that support should be given to various CCC projects and activities.

4.12   There has been a tendency for CCCs to develop first in Counties which lack a strong County museums service. The assistance and encouragement of AMCs has usually been a critical factor in establishing a CCC on a sound basis. The Area Museums Service for South-Eastern England (AMSSEE) has been particularly positive in its support for CCCs, with the result that only three Counties in its area (which stretches from Norfolk to Hampshire) are now without CCCs. Many CCCs choose to begin with very limited financial obligations on member authorities and museums. However, if they decide to appoint a countywide museums co-ordinator or peripatetic curator this will obviously have an impact on the funding requirement. As experience has shown that such appointments are highly beneficial to the effectiveness of a CCC, Area Museum Councils have tended to pump-prime such posts, but the major part of the on-going funding comes from local authorities.

4.13   The functions and activities of CCCs and Forums differ according to local circumstances. In the south-east the activities of various CCCs have included *inter alia*: reports on museum provision and publication of countywide development plans; agreements on collecting policies; provision of centralised storage space for collections; surveys of conservation needs and the establishment of a conservation laboratory; documentation projects for small publicity ventures; publication of a museum education plan and information relating museum collections to the National Curriculum; establishment of a County Heritage Trust to raise money for the purchase of exhibits; and the provision of training seminars. Some CCCs also offer grants to museums in their area.

4.14   It is important to emphasise the strategic role of CCCs. This is well demonstrated by the new Cornwall Committee. Although it met only three times in 1988–89, the Committee immediately set about adopting guidelines on Museum Registration and endorsed a draft 'policy towards museums' for consideration by individual District councils. CCCs can also support AMCs by encouraging various agencies to use their grants effectively to promote museum development. The London Museums Consultative Committee, for example, has produced funding guidelines which it has persuaded the London Tourist Board, the Greater London Arts Association and the London Boroughs Grants Unit to accept.

4.15 The CCCs have been especially helpful to the smaller independent museums in terms of professional support. Bearing in mind that local authorities are often the major funders of CCCs, this represents an important indirect subsidy to independent museums. A particularly encouraging trend in the last few years has been the establishment of curatorial advisory posts by County Councils such as Cumbria, Northumberland, Leicestershire and Lancashire, and by District Councils such as Ryedale and Ross & Cromarty. These authorities have recognised the importance of providing professional support to independent museums within their areas and we welcome the assistance this renders to the implementation of the MGCs Registration Scheme which we detail in Chapter 5. We should also note that these curatorial posts have not just been a drain on local authority resources, but they have enabled the independent museums to obtain additional help, both in kind and in grants from other organisations, because of the professional input.

4.16 While the services and facilities offered by both Area Museum Councils and Countywide Consultative Committees may appear fairly comprehensive, the Association of Independent Museums (AIM) has recently published a report titled *New Visions For Independent Museums in the UK* (1990) which identifies a gap in the market. The report states that 'it is increasingly clear that no independent museum is big enough to stand entirely alone. Even the largest (such as Beaulieu) are joined in consortia for marketing and other purposes and the evidence of The National Trust, English Heritage, and the grouping of commercial attractions under Madame Tussauds management, all reflect the benefits of belonging to *management* networks or consortia'. A key recommendation in the report is the establishment of functional management consortia involving both independent and local authority museums. Given the weaknesses of small museums the scope for forming consortia is large but a number of aspects are noted including: the need for information exchange networking using modern information technology; the need for educational networking in respect of developing cost effective education services for schools; and marketing and merchandising networks. A working party established by the National Economic Development Council has been considering a similar set of ideas which might extend the work of management consortia into such fields as financial and personnel services.

4.17 In broad terms we support appropriate linkages between museums on a regional and sub-regional basis. It is important, however, to avoid duplication of effort, and the MGC has agreed to take the lead in co-ordinating any new initiatives.

4.18 The particular situation in Northern Ireland deserves a separate mention at this point. The small number of local authority and independent museums has hitherto militated against the establishment of a formal support organisation for museums. However, with the encouragement of the MGC, the Northern Ireland Museums Advisory Committee (NIMAC) has recently been formed. In essence it is an embryonic AMC. A full-time development officer has been appointed through funding from the MGC and the Northern Ireland Education Department and museums in Northern Ireland, and a number of networking activities are being pursued.

4.19 The top priority for NIMAC is the development of a regional museums policy for Northern Ireland. A recent NIMAC discussion paper examined existing museums provision and noted that, in addition to the national museums (including Armagh Museum which is a constituent part of Ulster Museum), there are local authority museums at Enniskillen, Downpatrick, Derry City, Lisburn and Bangor. However, there is no regional museums service in most of County Antrim, County Londonderry or County Tyrone. NIMAC's approach is to encourage a limited number of regional museums services and to seek the maximum co-operation between local authorities to achieve this goal. It also sees specialist museums, display centres, small local museums, renovated industrial buildings and other heritage projects linking in to the framework of regional museums services. We applaud NIMAC's strategic thinking and RECOMMEND its establishment as a fully fledged AMC, with appropriate government funding.

Local Authorities and Independent Museums

4.20 The majority of UK museums started as the private collection of an individual or of a learned or historical society. Most of the first generation of 'independent' museums, which started in the late 18th and early 19th centuries, failed to survive or were taken over by local authorities in the Victorian period to form the basis of our major municipal collections today. A few of the original Society museums still survive, constitutionally independent but usually reliant on revenue funding from local authorities in order to sustain their current level of service. Examples include the Salisbury and South Wiltshire Museum; the Dorset County Museum and the Royal Cornwall Museum which are subsidised by Wiltshire, Dorset and Cornwall County Councils respectively.

4.21 Thus, independent museums are not a new phenomenon although it is important to note that the majority have been established in the last thirty years. The fact that many independent museums rely on local authority support is not always properly recognised outside the museum profession. For example, over 50% of the revenue funding for the independent Museum of East Anglian Life is derived from four local authorities. However, most independent museums receive grants from local authorities only sporadically, or at best on a year-to-year basis. If financial freedom is one of the advantages of an independent museum, the other side of the coin is financial frailty. Nearly all independent museums depend to a greater or lesser extent on income from admission charges, and inevitably this means that they are affected by external factors such as the weather, transport problems, restrictions on the number of educational visits or the state of the tourist trade, which in turn may depend on the vagaries of exchange rates. Given this essential frailness it is often difficult for independent museums to invest in specialist staff and in the behind-the-scenes facilities which are essential for the long-term preservation of the collections and their use by educational groups and researchers. This is where local authorities can be of the greatest assistance, providing on-going revenue support towards basic aspects of a museums service. They can also encourage improvements to the infrastructure and marketing of independent museums through providing challenge grants. Such support can be justified on the basis of their substantial contribution to the tourism and cultural amenities of a particular area.

4.22 A successful partnership must, of course, be based upon a sense of common purpose. One of the underlying problems holding back the development of The Boat Museum in Cheshire has been the lack of trust between the District Council and the Museum Trust. It is essential that a detailed plan for the museum's future be agreed at an early stage. Thereafter, it is important that good communications are maintained at all levels. Local authority members will often become nominated representatives on the Board of Management and it is important that they understand their responsibilities. Guidelines have recently been drawn up by the Museums Association (see Appendix C) and it is RECOMMENDED that all potential committee members of independent museums should be invited to indicate their willingness to be guided by the guidelines, and to acknowledge their corporate and personal liabilities under the museum's constitution before any offer of appointment is finalised. It is also important that all members of the local authority understand the responsibilities and priorities of one of their members who has been appointed to a museum trust.

4.23   We have already mentioned the difficult situation faced by independent museums which rely on local authority grants provided on a year-to-year basis. If a museum is prepared to draw-up a three year business plan (rolled forward annually) we see considerable advantages in a local authority indicating a willingness to provide financial support over a commensurate period. From the museum's point of view this would allow planning to proceed on a more coherent basis so long as there is sufficient flexibility in the arrangement for factors, such as inflation, to be taken into account. Several local authorities have found it both possible and advantageous to plan ahead in this way.

4.24   The Museum of Richmond is an independent local history museum devoted to Richmond, Ham, Petersham, and Kew in Surrey. It opened in October 1988 and is operated by the Museum of Richmond Company which is limited by guarantee and registered as a charity. In December 1986 a licence agreement was signed between the company and the London Borough of Richmond-upon-Thames. Under this agreement the local authority agreed to provide the museum premises plus heating, lighting and cleaning services for a notional sum. In addition, it undertook to provide for the cost of two members of staff (since revised to cover the cost of a curator and two part-time assistants) after the museum had been open to the public for two years. The company had to cover the capital expense of setting up the museum and had to raise money for the staffing costs until that part of the agreement came into effect. This challenge funding arrangement has proved successful. The local authority is now supporting the basic running costs of the museum and in return the company is looking after the Borough's historic artefact collection and provides a wide-ranging public service to local residents and tourists.

4.25 The arrangement between the London Borough of Richmond-upon-Thames and the Museum of Richmond Trust is exemplary in two respects. First, there is the financial forward planning and second, the existence of a formal written agreement between the two parties. We RECOMMEND that financial partnerships between local authorities and independent, armed services and university museums should always be subject to written agreements. One aspect of the Richmond arrangement may have to be reconsidered, and that is the question of the peppercorn rent. In future, local authorities will have to charge economic rents, and we trust that they will compensate by providing an appropriate level of grant support.

4.26 Regular local authority support towards the running costs of an independent museum need not result in the stifling of initiative with regard to plural funding. Abbot Hall Art Gallery and the Museum of Lakeland Life and Industry, Kendal, are independent museums run by a private charitable trust, the Lake District Art Gallery and Museum Trust. The premises occupied by the art gallery and the museum are rented from the South Lakeland District Council (on the basis of a full repairing lease of 99 years duration) by the Trust for a nominal sum. The Trust is proud of the fact that it has reduced the proportion of local authority support from 80% of the revenue budget 12 years ago to 30% in 1989–90. Moreover, it has been highly successful in raising money from private sources towards the cost of a major capital improvement programme. Notwithstanding these achievements the Trust justifiably feels that as the art gallery and museum provide a public service not available elsewhere within the county of Cumbria, let alone South Lakeland District, some degree of local authority core funding is both valid and necessary.

4.27 We mentioned in Chapter 3 that several independent museums in regular receipt of funds from local authorities actually started life as local authority museums. The benefits to a public authority of quasi-independent status lie chiefly in the opportunity to actively involve a broad spectrum of the local community in the running of the museum, and the greater potential for fund-raising in the private sector. On the other hand there may be disadvantages in the long-term arising from being distanced from the seat of political power and source of funding. Also, independent museums are often reliant on the enthusiasm of a few key trustees, who cannot be expected to be around for ever.

4.28 It would be a mistake of course to think about local authority support solely in terms of grants. At Abbot Hall for example, the publicity officer has the full support of the District Council's Tourism and Leisure Department; the grounds of the three museums are planted and cared for by the Parks Department; the Treasurers Department deals with the museum's staff PAYE; while the legal and personnel department are at their disposal. The District Council was also happy to act as an intermediary in a Private Treaty Sale transaction in 1988, because local authorities are referred to in 'Schedule 3' of the Inheritance Tax Act 1984, whereas independent museums are not. However, we RECOMMEND that Registered independent museums should be allowed to benefit from Private Treaty Sales in their own right.

4.29 The Ironbridge Gorge Museum is an independent charitable trust operating largely within the District of the Wrekin. The District Council does not operate a museums service of its own but it supports Ironbridge with a grant of some £7,500 per annum, nominally towards a Sites Warden. Just as important, however, are the various services which Wrekin District Council provides. The Council operates the Wrekin Tourism Association, a promotional organisation involving all local attractions, hotels and other interested bodies, and the support of this association is greatly appreciated by the museum as it enhances its marketing budget. In addition, the Council largely funds the museum's Park and Ride Service and also provides funding for a direct train link from Birmingham Central Station to Coalbrookdale – the home of the museum. The Council is also helpful in providing assistance to the museum in terms of landscaping and environmental improvements. This level of support from the District Council is to be welcomed but it has to be seen in the context of Ironbridge attracting a million visitors (1988), of whom 405,000 went through the museum's gates. Of this figure over half were staying in the locality and therefore bringing considerable benefits to the area. The museum itself spent £4m in 1988, much of it inside the local area. Taking these facts together, it is hardly surprising that Ironbridge Gorge Museum feels that for a modest investment the District Council is actually reaping a much higher reward from the indirect benefits of tourism, and the general appearance and image of the locality.

4.30 A number of independent museums receive support in kind from Local Education Authorities. Ironbridge Gorge Museum benefits from having two teachers on secondment from Shropshire County Council's Education Department, while the Greater

Manchester Museum of Science and Industry (GMMSI) has five teachers – four provided by the City of Manchester and one by the City of Salford. The strength of the GMMSI education service is that it is both an integral part of the museum, involved in all its activities through a project team system, and is closely involved with the local authorities. In consequence, it has been in a position to take the lead in curriculum development work associated with the National Curriculum, and in the in-service training of teachers. The museum benefits from the provision of excellent educational services while the local authority benefits through the provision of an educational resource of great value.

4.31 An increasing number of smaller independent museums receive professional support and advice from their colleagues in local authority museums. This is partly due to the introduction of the MGC's Registration Scheme and the arrangement whereby independent museums without a professionally qualified and/or experienced curator on the staff formally adopt a museum adviser. The majority of these advisers are from the local authority museum sector, some of them specifically employed to act in a peripatetic advisory capacity.

4.32 Local authorities can also assist independent museums through granting relief to charities on the Uniform Business Rate (UBR). Charities now receive a mandatory 80% relief on the UBR but local authorities have discretion to grant a further 20%. In view of the educational amenity provided by museums we RECOMMEND that all charitable and non-profit distributing independent museum premises should be allowed the full 100% relief on the UBR.

4.33 A characteristic of museums generally, but of the independent sector in particular, is that it is easier to find the money for starting a new museum than for running an existing one. The Miles Report noted how money or help in kind was available for a wide range of government sources such as the Development Agencies, Tourist Boards, the Manpower Services Commission (now the Training Agency) and the European Regional Development Fund. Unfortunately none of these bodies, which have done so much to help set up new museums, can help meet the running costs afterwards. The Scottish Mining Museum for example, having extricated itself from the tangled transition of Community Programme to Employment Training, now depends almost exclusively on a consortium of three local authorities (one

Regional, two Districts) for its revenue. Sustaining the interest of the three supporting councils is a constant marketing exercise for the museum. Efforts to recruit other Councils' support through the Convention of Scottish Local Authorities have only been partially successful even though the museum has a national function. However, in common with their approach towards similar industrial museums in Scotland, the Regions take the view that they need to see evidence of government support through direct revenue funding, on some appropriate scale, before they can justify contributing themselves to any organisation outside their respective areas. For its part, the Scottish Office takes the view that museums like the Scottish Mining Museum are the responsibility of regions and Districts, since this is where the sites are, the government share being met through the Revenue Support Grant. It has been suggested that one method of addressing the situation might be the setting up of a Scottish industrial museum network together with a central reference point. Such an arrangement would acknowledge and support the important function of industrial museums. The absence of any financial backing seems unfortunately to have acted as a deterrent to any significant progress on setting up such a network.

4.34   It is very clear that most independent museums will require assistance from local authorities at one time or another. Indeed, local authorities are an important 'long-stop' if an independent museum runs into serious difficulty. It was not so long ago that the independent Gladstone Pottery Museum deservedly won the Museum of the Year Award. Yet in 1989 the museum had to be rescued from a financial crisis by Stoke-on-Trent District Council. We welcome this sort of commitment from local authorities. However, not all museums will be regarded as of sufficient importance to be bailed out in this way, so it is incumbent on all those, (including local authorities), who provide financial assistance towards the setting-up of an independent museum, to seek advice on the future viability of the museum from the relevant Area Museum Council at the earliest possible opportunity.

Local Authorities and Armed Services Museums

4.35   The regimental and corps museums are the most numerous category of armed services museums. With few exceptions, each museum is constituted as a charitable trust. The regimental museums of the Regular Army – the Infantry and the Cavalry –

have strong territorial links and this factor has encouraged links between regimental and local authority museums. Nearly 40 regimental museums (about one-third of the total), including those of all but two of the Cavalry regiments, are now managed within local authority museums. The corps of the army are the specialist arms of the service and none has a strong territorial link. As a result they have rarely been candidates for management arrangements with local authority museums, though some have received periodic local authority funding support.

4.36 Apart from the regimental and corps museums of the regular army there is a large group of collections reflecting the history of local militia, yeomanry and volunteer forces. Most are now established as trusts but they are not authorised to receive staffing or premises costs from the Ministry of Defence. It is therefore highly desirable that such collections should find appropriate parent bodies such as local authority museums. In some cases this has been achieved through the formation of county military museums. Good examples include the Somerset Military Museum at Taunton (part of Somerset County Museums Service) and the Sussex Combined Services Museum which has a management arrangement with Eastbourne Borough Council.

4.37 The idea that regimental collections should be transferred on loan to local authority museums has been warmly supported by the Army Museums Ogilby Trust for many years. This arrangement has a number of advantages. On the one hand the regimental museum trustees retain ownership of the collection, are involved to a greater or lesser extent with policy making, and have the opportunity to continue providing specialist advice and information relating to the history of the regiment and its collections. Local authority involvement, on the other hand, brings the collection within the ambit of professional museum care and interpretation as well as making it accessible to a wider public. There are numerous examples of such partnerships. Some of the most successful recent developments include the newly opened Norfolk Regimental Museum, now part of Norfolk County Museums Service; the County and Regimental Museum in Preston, where Lancashire County Museum Service houses collections relating to four County Regiments; and the Museum of the Manchesters in Ashton-under-Lyne, a museum developed by Tameside Museums Service to house the collection of the Manchester Regiment. One of the most attractive features of this link between local authority and regimental museums is the opportunity to place military collections within a broader historical, social and multi-cultural context.

4.38 In commending such arrangements, the MGC's recent report titled *The Museums of the Armed Services* (1990) offered some sound practical advice. It stressed the importance of discussing joint responsibilities at the outset so that each party understands the other's expectations. Policy relating to matters such as acquisition, display, and loans should all be discussed prior to a written agreement being drawn up. The loan agreement should be accompanied by a schedule of the items transferred to the local authority, and the right for either side to withdraw from the agreement should be subject to a proper period of notice. The report also recommended that careful consideration should be given to the relationship between the object collection and the regimental archive and library. If they are to be kept together, the local authority must be able to provide adequate housing and specialist staff to provide an enquiry service equal to that provided by the regiment. If archives remain at Regimental Headquarters, thought should be given to establishing joint procedures for research, access and enquiry. At the end of the day, the success of loan agreements usually depends on an active relationship between the regiment and the museum. The keystone of this relationship should be ideally a joint advisory committee composed of regimental museum trustees and local authority representatives.

4.39 The level of support provided by the Ministry of Defence to non-national military museums is generally inadequate to meet the basic running costs, so any local authority assistance, whether in cash or in kind, is highly appreciated. The fact that the City of Cardiff has recently increased its level of subsidy by a significant amount to The Welch Regiment Museum of the Royal Regiment of Wales is particularly encouraging, given the financial uncertainties generated by the introduction of the community charge. We RECOMMEND that local authorities should continue to support armed services museums and seek ways to assist the preservation of publicly owned military collections which are currently without any professional oversight. The MGC's report on museums of the armed services also suggested that those responsible for collections in Territorial Army centres should seriously consider loaning the bulk of the collection to a local museum if they can see no long-term solution to the physical problems which they face. We concur with this view.

Local Authorities and University Museums

4.40 Many university museums and collections are in a precarious position chiefly as a result of successive years of under-funding and under-staffing. The funding of a university's collections depends of course on the total funding it receives from the Universities Funding Council (UFC). The UFC does not earmark subsidies to university museums although a number of the most important collections are recognised as non-departmental special factors and the total funding of the university includes an allowance for this. The UFC may recognise the importance of university museums and collections in terms of teaching and research but it is unlikely to contemplate the funding of any community role. This is where local authorities can provide much needed assistance. However, in spite of the fact that most universities are located in or near large centres of population and their museums represent a valuable educational and recreational resource, local authorities tend to take the view that universities should be solely responsible for the adequate funding of their museums and collections.

4.41 Of eight museums in the City of Cambridge, six are university museums and two are small independent institutions. Only two of the university museums receive any regular financial support from local authorities towards their general running costs. In both cases this support comprises grants to extend public access at weekends. Essentially therefore, the University is providing, from its own resources, a public museums service for the City of Cambridge and its environs. Although these university museums are open to the public, often for limited hours, free of charge, they are primarily institutions for university teaching and research. Without additional resources they cannot provide all the local facilities which the public expects of a County or City museums service.

4.42 The Fitzwilliam Museum, Cambridge, currently receives a grant of £21,000 on a year-to-year basis from Cambridge City Council (unchanged since 1987) and £1,590 from South Cambridgeshire District Council towards the cost of warding the galleries at weekends. This support is welcome but it represents some 62.4% of the costs of opening at weekends and 11.2% of the costs of opening the museum from Tuesday to Sunday. It is a totally inadequate contribution when one considers that the Fitzwilliam welcomes some 225,000 visitors a year in a town of 100,000 inhabitants. Many of these visitors are tourists who bring money and trade to the region. Yet for lack of £70,000 or so a year, the Fitzwilliam cannot keep all its galleries open on weekdays.

4.43   It is noteworthy that, in Cambridgeshire, such local authority support as is available for recurrent museum expenditure comes from the District Councils. Of the County's six District Councils, however, only Peterborough can be said to provide an adequate museums service. County Council support is limited to the employment of one County Museums Officer, provision of the Cromwell Museum in Huntingdon, payment of very small capital grants to individual museums, and the secondment of a teacher to the Fitzwilliam Museum on a 4 days per week basis. As a result of this pitiful level of local authority support for museums, an unfair burden rests upon the University, and the City and County as a whole are inadequately provided with museum facilities.

4.44   The Cambridge situation has its parallels at Oxford, although, to be fair, Oxfordshire County Council provides a comprehensive County museums service which includes the Museum of Oxford. The City Council's annual grant of £1,000 to the Ashmolean Museum towards opening the galleries on Sunday afternoons can only be regarded as derisory.

4.45   The potential of university museums as educational institutions, especially in the light of the National Curriculum, deserves recognition by Local Education Authorities. We have already mentioned the seconded teacher at the Fitzwilliam Museum. This has been a very successful arrangement but demand far out-runs supply and the whole project is very hand-to-mouth. A small grant from Eastern Arts has helped to provide teaching materials, while the Friends of the Fitzwilliam provide a small band of volunteer helpers for educational activities. The future is uncertain because the seconded teacher is available for only two more years. The education service would obviously benefit from a longer-term commitment by the Local Education Authority. The Fitzwilliam needs its own teacher, and an additional education liaison officer could exploit the potential of all the museums in Cambridge.

4.46   A similar need is apparent at Oxford where the Ashmolean provides an excellent educational service purely through the efforts of volunteers. Oxfordshire Education Authority's involvement with university museums has been limited to modest assistance such as the printing of educational materials for the Pitt Rivers Museum. By way of contrast, the Manchester Museum is in the fortunate position of having had its education staff funded by the City of Manchester Education Committee since 1916. Premises are provided and maintained by the university for this purpose and there are no recharging arrangements between the university and local authority. In 1981 the City of Manchester spent £80,000 on upgrading the classroom facilities at the museum. However, the education staff, which at one time numbered five teachers and ancillary staff, currently comprises only three teachers and the City of Manchester's financial difficulties raise questions about the future of the service.

4.47 Manchester Museum is unusual in having received regular local authority support from 1895 to 1986 when the Greater Manchester Council was abolished as a result of local government re-organisation. This support was by no means confined to education. By 1986 the Greater Manchester Council (GMC) was contributing 41% of the museum's revenue expenditure in addition to the City's support for the education service. There were frequent inputs of capital expenditure, for a museum extension in 1977 and for a gallery redevelopment programme. The provision of both revenue and capital expenditure by the local authority persuaded the university to match that input and there were many achievements resulting from this partnership. More generally, local authority involvement, particularly that of the GMC, gave the museum a wider political and geographical basis than it would have enjoyed under the university alone. Furthermore, the local authority's financial input meant that within the university attitudes to the museum were probably more sympathetic, in that the museum was not adjudged to be 'robbing' the university of money from the university's main function of teaching and research. There is no doubt that the benefits of local authority support to the Manchester Museum were considerable and are greatly missed.

4.48 The partnership arrangement, whereby the university supports the collection resource and its management, teaching and research while the local authority supports the museum's public services, is an attractive one. It should be remembered that the government's Standard Spending Assessment allows for the provision of museums services even if a local authority does not operate a museum itself. Where university and local authority museums exist in the same area their collections usually complement rather than duplicate one another. Given these circumstances we RECOMMEND that local authorities should recognise university museums' contribution to the cultural and educational amenity by making available an appropriate level of recurrent financial help. In return for this investment university museums should strive to make themselves accessible by improved opening hours and publicity; through education programmes, temporary exhibitions and special events; and by providing better public facilities including provision for the disabled people. It would not be unreasonable for local authorities making substantial financial contributions to university museums to expect to have one or two elected members on the museums' governing bodies.

4.49   We have signalled our approval for partnerships, but there are occasions when local authorities might need to consider a greater financial involvement than simply providing grants towards a university museum's public services. Following withdrawal of financial support by University College, Swansea in 1986, Wales's oldest museum, that of the Royal Institution of South Wales, and better known as Swansea Museum, had to fight a long battle against closure. A Working Group of interested parties, including Swansea City Council, was established to consider both short and long-term strategies. It was apparent from the outset that the collections held by the City Council and the Swansea Museum are entirely complementary. The City Council already operates an art gallery and a maritime and industrial museum whereas the strengths of the Swansea Museum collections lie in the natural sciences and local history and archaeology. Happily, a solution has been found. Swansea City Council has agreed to accept the museum building from the college and the collections from the Royal Institution. Swansea Museum will now become part of the Council's existing museums and galleries service while the Royal Institution of South Wales will continue to provide active support for the new management. Swansea City Council is not without its own financial difficulties, so it is to be warmly congratulated for rescuing one of Wales's outstanding museum collections.

4.50   A similar crisis has afflicted Bangor Museum and Art Gallery. The University College of North Wales decided in 1989 that it could no longer meet the running costs of the museum. The Council of Museums in Wales was requested by the University to carry out a feasibility study on the future of the institution. The most attractive options featured financial support from local authorities in the area. Gwynedd County Council already operates a joint museums and archive service but the museum element is modest. A museum development officer advises all types of museums in Gwynedd and has responsibility for certain specialist museums including Beaumaris Gaol and the Lloyd George

Museum at Llanystumdwy. Arfon District Council, on the other hand, does not provide any sort of museums service. Neither Gwynedd nor Arfon have provided revenue funding to Bangor Museum in the past, yet the museum's collections are of regional importance, especially its archaeology and social history collections. The only regular supporter of Bangor Museum has been the City of Bangor, now a Community Council, which until recently provided a grant of £1,000 a year. In 1990–91 however, Gwynedd provided £10,000 and Arfon £5,000 towards the running costs of the museum pending discussions as to its future. As with Swansea, a rescue package involving local authorities is being considered. This would involve Gwynedd taking responsibility for the management of the museum on the basis that they will find two-thirds of the running costs while Arfon contributes the other third. The University College of North Wales would provide the building at a peppercorn rent while the Council of Museums in Wales would assist through establishing a 'subsidised curator' post. Such a solution would be highly satisfactory and reminds us yet again of the crucial role of local authorities.

4.51   We have received a number of submissions from university curators suggesting that they would welcome a greater involvement with local authority museums and their staff. Informal contacts are said to be good but a formal structure is felt to be desirable. An example of a successful arrangement seems to be the Oxfordshire Museums Advisory Committee (OMAC) which was set up under the aegis of the Area Museum Council to draw together the county, university and independent museums. Good relations have been formed between the county museums service and the participating university museums, and tangible benefits such as a countywide publicity leaflet have resulted. We RECOMMEND that all university museums should take steps to establish more formal lines of communication with the wider museum community.

Local Authorities and National Museums

4.52   All museums are custodians of the national heritage and this fact needs to be recognised in the relationship between local authorities and national museums funded by central government. Some national museums have stronger traditions of involvement with local museums than others. To some extent, there has been greater involvement where national museums have been 'national' in terms of serving a particular part of the UK. The National

Museum of Wales, for example, has operated an 'affiliation scheme' for local museums in Wales since the 1920s, though its importance has diminished since the creation of the Council of Museums in Wales. In Northern Ireland there are very few local museums, but the Ulster Museum and the Ulster Folk and Transport Museum have traditionally exercised a pastoral role and are active and subscribing members of the newly established Northern Ireland Museums Advisory Committee. Several national museums including the Victoria and Albert (V&A) Museum, the British Museum and the National Gallery have long offered training opportunities for local museum staff in specialist areas such as security and conservation. We welcome the Science Museum's recent initiative in establishing a training course for museum staff wishing to specialise in the conservation of industrial collections, and its recent decision to designate a senior member of staff as External Affairs Co-ordinator. We commend the National Army Museum for its continuing provision of training courses for curators of regimental collections. In addition to the more formal training opportunities, it would be beneficial to all parties if more exchanges and secondments could take place between national and local authority museums' staff. We welcome the V&A's recent long-term exchange of members of staff with Brighton Polytechnic, and hope that this opportunity can also be extended to local museums. Most local authority museum curators will take advantage of the MGC's local museums purchase grant funds at one time or another and we welcome the continued involvement of staff at the Science and V&A Museums in the administration of these grant schemes.

4.53   We attach particular importance to the need to make the national museums' collections available to as wide a public as possible. The loan of material from national museum collections on both a long-term and a short-term basis for exhibition purposes is an activity we would seek to encourage. Such loans are costly in staff-time for national museums and we recognise the staffing difficulties that many of them currently face. We would urge local authority museums to be reasonable in their requirements of the national collections which are increasingly burdened by requests for large numbers of items, not all of which may be needed in the planned exhibitions. Equally, we would urge national museums to resist any pressure to introduce charges for loans to museums other than reimbursement for the costs involved in transporting items. We regret the fact that the Royal Armouries has recently decided to levy such charges. We would also urge the national museums to be more flexible in their negotiations on the number of couriers required and for how long, to help to justify the expense to the museums which have to afford the cost.

4.54 Some national museums still offer travelling exhibitions to local authority museums, but there has never been adequate compensation for the loss of the V&A Circulation Department. In the aftermath of the demise of this touring programme, the British Museum was given extra funding for touring, but it has been able to circulate very few prime exhibitions, like the 'Chinese Bronzes' exhibition, which contain major objects. It has not the advantage of the collection which the V&A had built up specifically for touring, so it tends to circulate prints and other two-dimensional material to a few secure venues. The Science Museum's Loan Exhibition Scheme proved popular throughout the late 1960s and 1970s but in 1981, due to cutbacks in staffing and resources, the exhibitions were transferred to the Tyne and Wear Museums Service who currently operate the scheme on an agency basis. The majority of the exhibitions are now outdated in their presentation and are literally worn out, and so some exhibitions are being withdrawn from circulation and the future of the scheme is under review. Against this background any new initiatives are to be welcomed, such as the National Gallery's proposal to tour its 'Artist's Eye' exhibition. More could be done, but additional government funds are required for the purpose. So far as local authority museums and galleries are concerned it is obviously important that they have the appropriate temporary exhibition facilities to handle these loan exhibitions. Security and environmental conditions in particular must be adequate. While local authorities can be expected to find some of the capital expenditure required it is important that challenge funds from central government are made available. The MGC's capital grants fund needs enhancing if the provision of temporary exhibition areas is to be added to its terms of reference. A joint initiative with the Arts Council might be contemplated.

4.55 While there is an obvious need for national museums to make their collections more widely available through touring exhibitions, it should be recognised that many of them have opened significant outstations in recent years. Several of the outstations have been the result of collaboration with local authorities, and two of them have won the Museum of the Year Award which places special emphasis on public services. The first outstation to achieve this honour (in 1988) was the National Museum of Photography, Film and Television (NMPFT), a branch of the Science Museum.

From the outset, Bradford City Council provided political and officer support and practical assistance towards establishing the museum which opened in 1983. Today, the NMPFT continues to enjoy a particularly positive and harmonious relationship with the local authority. Its modern building is leased at a peppercorn rent and the local authority provides six full-time teaching staff based permanently at the museum. The NMPFT attracts almost a million visitors annually, and this success is in no small measure aided by Bradford's own positive tourism marketing strategy in which the museum figures largely. The NMPFT has a number of exciting plans for the future and it is no surprise that Bradford is keen to assist these developments.

4.56 A more recent winner of the Museum of the Year Award (1989) is the National Portrait Gallery's outstation at Bodel-wyddan Castle, North Wales. Clwyd County Council provided the 'framework', in other words, the building itself and the costs of restoration; the costs of decoration, carpets and curtains, fixtures and fittings; the warding costs, maintenance of the display, and supervision of environmental conditions; car parks, restaurant and other facilities; and the provision of promotional material. The Gallery provided the exhibits and design and curatorial expertise: approximately 100 Nineteenth Century portraits restored and reframed as necessary; the design of the rooms in which the portraits are displayed; the labels and accompanying booklet; educational back-up; and assistance with the provision of the exhibitions programme.

4.57 A number of other national museums, including the Tate Gallery and the V&A Museum, have been considering new outstations. The support of local authorities will almost certainly be critical to their realisation and future success. Outstations have been considered in terms of large investments in new operations, which must limit their number and, therefore, their effectiveness as methods of making national collections more widely available. We would urge an alternative, involving a closer collaboration between the national museum and the local museum, in order to build on existing staff and buildings, where such facilities already exist, for mutual benefit. A national museum might have a semi-permanent relationship with three or four such partners for the cost of administering a single outstation on a greenfield site, and be able to circulate major long-term exhibitions to each in turn.

4.58 We have mentioned the way in which the National Museum of Photography, Film and Television has benefitted from the secondment of teachers by Bradford. Other national museums have also collaborated with local authorities to establish education services. One of the oldest and most comprehensive must be the National Museum of Wales (NMW) Schools Service which was established in 1949. This service comprises: a loan service, travelling workshop, museum based activities and visits; lectures and special visits; field excursions and in-service training courses for teachers. Originally the Service was jointly funded by the NMW and all the local education authorities in Wales. At the present time only five out of the eight local education authorities contribute to the Service. If any more drop out, the future of the Service could be placed in jeopardy. We would urge Local Education Authorities in Wales to continue or renew their support for the NMW Schools Service. Apart from the facilities mentioned above, school parties receive free entry into all NMW branches. This tradition of free entry for school parties is an important one and we are glad that it is being honoured by those national museums in London which have recently introduced admission charges for the general public.

5. Managing Museums – Recent Developments

5.1 Having reviewed the various ways in which local authorities relate to museums, we need to examine how a number of external factors have influenced the operation of local authority museums.

Registration of Museums

5.2 The MGC's Registration Scheme has two main objectives: first, to establish minimum requirements for a museum in terms of its constitution, collecting policy and curatorial care, and thereby contribute to the raising of museum standards in the United Kingdom (UK); and second, to enable a museum to demonstrate, to the public and potential funding agencies, that it is worthy of support. Following the successful pilot scheme undertaken in the North of England Museum Service area in 1986, it was decided that Registration should be implemented throughout the UK. The phased programme of implementation is based on Area Museum Council (AMC) areas and the first round of Registration is due for completion in 1992. At the time of writing, we are therefore approximately two-thirds of the way through the initial implementation process. Registered museums will be asked to renew their applications every five years, although general progress will be monitored on an annual basis.

5.3 Registration is a voluntary scheme but there are significant benefits arising from participation. First, a Registered museum is eligible for grants and subsidised services from the MGC and AMCs, while other funding organisations have agreed to consider Registration as an important factor when making awards from their own grant schemes. Second, the achievement of Registered Status offers the opportunity for a museum to publicise itself both as an organisation which provides a basic range of public services and as a suitable repository for museum-worthy material. These incentives, taken together with the fact that Registration is chiefly concerned with establishing a policy framework (rather than setting standards which involve an immediate and major financial outlay) have resulted in applications from over 90% of existing AMC members, including most local authority museums. To date, no local authority museums have been rejected by the MGC Registration Committee. At the time of writing 65% have achieved full registration status, while 25% have provisional status which means that improvements have to be made within a given timescale, but the museum remains eligible for financial assistance. The remaining museums are awaiting decisions by the Registration Committee.

5.4 To meet the criteria set out in the Registration guidelines, (see Appendix D), local authority museums have to provide evidence relating to their constitutional basis and financial viability. This has not generally been a problem, although the Registration Committee has been concerned on occasions when local authorities seem to be setting aside too little in their budgets for vital aspects of a museum's work such as conservation. There has also been the need, on occasion, to formalise management agreements, for example, between local authorities and Regimental Museum Trustees whose collections are housed in local authority museums.

5.5 An important requirement of Registration is the submission of an acquisition and disposal policy which is in accord with the Registration guidelines. Many local authority museums have taken the opportunity to revise existing policies while others have produced policies for the first time. We noted in Chapter 2 that Registration requires museums to take account of the acquisition policies of other institutions with similar interests. This has stimulated a number of local and regional collecting agreements, for example, archaeological collecting agreements between museums in Yorkshire and Humberside. We RECOMMEND that AMCs and Countywide Consultative Committees/Forums should work together to encourage collecting agreements between museums wherever appropriate. These agreements would provide the framework for further initiatives such as joint storage projects and the rationalisation of existing collections. The Registration guidelines cover the disposal of collections in some detail. They state that there should be a strong presumption against disposal. In those cases where a museum is free to dispose of an item, and where there are sound curatorial reasons for taking this course of action, a standard procedure for disposal is laid down in the guidelines. Any proceeds from the sale of accessioned material should be applied solely for the benefit of the museum collections, normally the purchase of new exhibits. Museums contravening the Registration guidelines run the risk of being de-registered, although there is a procedure for appeals.

5.6 The publication of an acquisition and disposal policy is only one part of a broader approach to collection management. The Registration Scheme requires museums to develop policies towards the documentation, conservation and preservation of their collections. A minimum standard is laid down for documentation which requires museums to have an adequate system in place. It also requires museums to state if any documentation backlog exists and, if so, to set out a timetable for its elimination. At least 25% of local authority museums have significant documentation backlogs, although the use of Manpower Services Commission schemes, up until a few years ago, helped to alleviate the position. The size of the backlogs has often been a reason for museums being granted provisional rather than full Registration. Such is the problem for some local authority museums such as Plymouth and Exeter, that they have decided to reduce temporarily the level of public services in order to release staff to tackle the matter. We have also noticed a significant number of advertisements for documentation officer posts during the last two years. It is important that all local authority museums should be provided with sufficient resources to meet the Registration standard for documentation. Quite apart from considerations relating to audit and security, if a museum does not know what is has in its collections it can hardly claim to be using them for the public benefit.

5.7 The requirements of Registration in respect of public services have caused few problems for local authority museums especially as the guidelines do not lay down minimum standards. Most of them have been able to satisfy the Registration Committee that they provide an appropriate range of public services relating to the interpretation of their collections. They have also been able to claim a reasonable range of visitor facilities appropriate to the scale, location and nature of their museums, and their opening hours have generally been adequate. However, there may be a need for more detailed guidance in this area (see 5.9).

5.8 Finally, the Registration guidelines state that a museum's governing body 'has a special obligation to ensure that the museum has staff sufficient in both number and kind to ensure that the museum is able to meet its responsibilities'. The Scheme recognises that the size of the staff and its nature will depend on the size of the museum, its collections, and its responsibilities. However, it would be wholly exceptional for a local authority museum to be registered if it did not employ the services of a professionally trained and/or experienced curator. It is also expected that the senior museum professional should normally be allowed direct access to the appropriate local authority committee, at least when estimates are presented and museum policy discussed. We are glad that these stipulations have created few problems for local authorities. The support which local authority museum curators provide to independent museums when acting as curatorial advisers has already been gratefully acknowledged in Chapter 4.

5.9 The Registration Scheme is considered by many to be one of the major museum developments of recent years. The MGC is grateful for the support it has received from the Museums Association, the Association of Independent Museums, AMCs and the Local Authority Associations, both in formulating and implementing the Scheme. However, we are not blind to ways in which Registration can be extended and improved. The following areas of museum activity need careful consideration when the Registration guidelines are next revised:

(i) standards relating to the conservation of collections, especially environmental monitoring;

(ii) enhanced documentation standards;

(iii) standards relating to security;

(iv) standards relating to public services, for example, the formal adoption of policies towards education and disabled access. We shall also need to take note of other work in this area, for example, the Tourist Board Visitor Attractions Code;

(v) guidelines for mission statements and forward plans.

5.10 We should not forget that Registration is concerned primarily with *minimum* standards. This does not mean that the MGC is uninterested in promoting *higher* standards. With financial assistance from the Office of Arts and Libraries, it has recently embarked on a standards development programme which is concentrating, in the first instance, on establishing optimum standards for the care of different types of museum material. At the time of writing, four standards are being developed for archaeological, biological, geological and industrial collections. These standards are being drawn up with the assistance of expert groups, including representatives from specialist museums groups, national museums and AMCs. The draft standards will be subject to a period of consultation before being published. They should become a basic standard reference point for museums, for example, when developing performance measures or creating new storage facilities.

Forward Plans, Measurement of Performance and Annual Report

5.11   As we have seen, the MGC's Registration Scheme is helping to create a policy framework for museum development. It is only one step further for museums to formulate comprehensive forward plans, and the MGC has funded *The Forward Planning Handbook* (to be published in 1991) which aims to assist this process. Forward plans (or corporate plans) should create a sense of direction by setting out the objectives, the priorities and the programme for the museums service. The objectives will naturally expand upon the fundamental purpose of museums as enshrined in the Museums Association's definition of a museum. The plans are typically devised on the basis of a three-year rolling programme and should incorporate appropriate performance measures. All staff should be involved in the development of the plan to instil a sense of 'ownership' and commitment. Such plans are standard for national museums and a number of local authority museums are beginning to follow suit. It is likely in future that many grant-giving bodies, such as AMCs, will require forward plans before allocating funds. In other words, before an AMC grant-aids the purchase of, say, showcases, it will want to see the bid in the context of a comprehensive display programme which in turn will be informed by the museum's marketing policy and its overall mission statement.

5.12   The measurement of a museum's performance can only be meaningful if it is placed in the context of a museum's forward plan. We commend the Museums Association (MA) and Association of Independent Museums (AIM) policy on performance measurement (1990) which states that 'The review of performance through the qualitative and quantitative measurement of outputs and inputs should be an integral part of the management process as a means of maximising all available resources.' It continues by suggesting that target standards relating to the key areas of curation, communication and operation are likely to be developed from the museum's forward plan, and they should be agreed by the governing body. It also makes the point that target standards will vary between museums depending on their objectives as well as their size, type and resources.

5.13 The Hampshire County Museums Service (HCMS) approach towards performance measurement follows the MA/AIM policy and is firmly based on the premise that performance review should be related to the attainment of clear objectives. The HCMS planning has a focus on the medium term (2–5 years) and consists of six main elements:

(i) Statement of Purpose.

(ii) Service Plan: a definition of objectives (with a likely currency of several years, often longer) and specific tasks which lead to the attainment of objectives, to be continually reviewed at an appropriate level of detail.

(iii) Acquisition Policy. To be reviewed at least every five years, with some unclear areas requiring review sooner.

(iv) Marketing Plan. This exists because of the operational need to highlight marketing and 'build' it into HCMS thinking.

(v) Personal Work Programmes. These attempt to harmonise the individual, the task, and the resources. They are intended to be the basis on which individual performance management and appraisal is developed.

(vi) Department Budget. This has been re-cast to make it relate more closely to the Service Plan and provide better feed-back to managers.

5.14 There are two complementary approaches to performance management. First, there is the performance of a service as outlined for example in *Managing Services Effectively – Performance Review* (Audit Commission, 1989). Second, is the performance of individuals as outlined for example in *Management of Performance, a managers guide* (The Society of Chief Personnel Officers, 1989). Whether one is talking about one or the other, two issues are fundamental to museum services: how to measure quality and how to measure outcomes, as distinct from outputs.

5.15 In the field of collection management it should be possible to measure quality and outcomes quite objectively. For example the following outputs might be measured:

(i) Achievement of an acquisition policy.

(ii) Environmental control related to agreed target standards.

(iii) Conservation and documentation programmes similarly quantified.

In these examples, outputs equate with outcomes in the sense that they all contribute to the ultimate objective, namely the better care of collections.

5.16 Measuring quality of performance in relation to public services can be more difficult. In some cases, however, it is possible to show that the achievement of an objective inevitably improves quality. For example, if the objective is to 'improve the effectiveness of the existing travelling exhibition service', tasks might include the provision of supporting educational material which allow schools to make more effective use of the exhibitions; and the establishment of a mechanism for advising appropriate schools of the availability of exhibitions and how they can make use of them. The objective is qualitative but vague. However, the tasks specify what elements of quality are actually going to be provided and it would be simple to measure the performance of those tasks.

5.17 Most museums use visitor figures as a performance measure. They will start to be useful as indicators of performance only if the method used to count visitors is reliable. Once this reliability has been achieved, performance can be evaluated over a period of years. Attendance figures can be affected, of course, by external factors such as a downturn in the tourist business. Comparisons with figures achieved by similar institutions can help to establish an appropriate context for an individual museum's performance. In order to evaluate the quality of the visitor experience it is vital that museums should carry out regular, consistent and validated market research. Visitor surveys can establish, for example, the frequency of repeat visits to a museum and the average length of time that people stay. Audience research can also investigate the reasons why people do *not* visit a particular museum. All this is important so that a museum can find out if it is satisfying visitors in the way it intended.

5.18 While comparisons between quantified measures and quantified targets are appropriate for some aspects of museum work (assuming quality standards can be agreed, as, for example, in documentation); other aspects such as scholarship are more difficult to evaluate. It would be simple to establish performance measures for scholarship in terms of the number of articles published, the number of lectures given, or the number of requests for information from researchers. However, we are not convinced by this approach. In our view the quality of scholarship as represented, for example, in publications and museum displays is best evaluated by some system of peer review.

5.19 To sum up, we RECOMMEND that all museums should develop forward plans and utilise related performance indicators on a selective basis. Quantified measures should be compared with quantified targets wherever possible but a more sophisticated approach is required to evaluate the quality of performance in many areas of museum work. More detailed guidance on performance measures for local authority museums can be found in the Audit Commission's report *The Road to Wigan Pier? – Managing local authority museums and art galleries* (1991).

5.20 As further evidence of accountability we also RECOMMEND that all local authority museums should publish reports on a regular, and preferably annual, basis. These reports should contain financial information relating to the service together with a detailed account of its main activities. The publication of annual reports was once fairly common among local authority museums but with the exception of a few institutions such as the Passmore Edwards Museum Service, Newham, and the Winchester Museums Service, the tradition has died away in recent years. The new emphasis on accountability makes the revival of this tradition imperative. Attractively produced annual reports can also be useful in the effective marketing of a museums service.

Marketing

5.21 The creation of a marketing plan should be one of the more important action plans to arise from the museum's forward plan. Useful advice about devising a marketing strategy can be found in *The Forward Planning Handbook.* In this publication, marketing is defined as 'the management process which confirms the mission of a museum or gallery and is then responsible for the efficient identification, anticipation and satisfaction of the needs of its users'. It is important that a museum should begin by establishing its 'mission'. A marketing plan can then be produced with the following elements:

(i) An assessment of users and non-users of the museum.

(ii) A judgement of the operational opportunities and constraints imposed on the museum.

(iii) A forecast of the quantity and quality of the experience it plans to offer.

(iv) A policy detailing what publications, retailing and catering services are appropriate.

(v) A promotion of the museum's services, including advertising and customer care training.

(vi) A timetable with a tight time-scale.

(vii) A budget which forecasts both income and expenditure.

(viii) Regular re-assessment.

5.22 Marketing is clearly a fundamental part of the management process and it is highly desirable that museums should have access to specialist marketing advice. We RECOMMEND that whenever possible local authority museums should employ designated marketing managers possibly on a shared basis. In addition, we note the advice of marketing specialists that museums should aim to spend at least 10% of their budgets on marketing. We further RECOMMEND that AMCs should consider the appointment of marketing advisers on the pattern of the Scottish Museums Council. AMCs should also aim to increase the proportion of grant-aid currently allocated to marketing in order to encourage more activity on the part of local authority museums.

5.23 There is no doubt that the MGC/OAL marketing scheme which commenced in 1988 has raised consciousness about marketing and its potential. Over a three year period, grants totalling some £335,000 have assisted a wide variety of marketing projects. A thousand museums across the UK have been affected by the scheme and over 600 have participated in long-term projects. Some of the most successful projects have been the regional marketing exercises co-ordinated by AMCs.

5.24 The 'Museums Alive!' project, for example organised by the Yorkshire and Humberside Museums Council (YHMC) aimed to increase public and media awareness; to elucidate the importance of museums; and to increase the number of visitors within the region. Specific objectives included the provision of training workshops in marketing for the region's professional and voluntary curators; the production of a series of publications highlighting co-ordinated events taking place in the region's museums in 1989 (Museums Year); and the provision of regular information to national, regional and local press, radio and television. Starting from a very low threshold of marketing awareness, with very few local authority museums having earmarked marketing budgets, 'Museums Alive!' proved a considerable success both in terms of improved visitor numbers to the region's museums and increased longer-term marketing activity. Evidence for the latter was the willingness of all YHMC members to contribute financially to the production and distribution of a second 'Museums Alive' booklet in 1990. The broad coverage offered by such a joint initiative was seen to be excellent value for money. We RECOMMEND that museums should collaborate on joint marketing initiatives and seek support from Area Museum Councils and Regional Tourist Boards.

Developed Management and Staffing Structures

5.25 The Audit Commission has recommended that four changes in the financial regime of local authorities will help to achieve better financial management:

(i) ensure that financial and management responsibilities are aligned so that managers who make decisions are responsible for the financial consequences and more senior managers supervise their results;

(ii) adapt ground rules so that each manager has clear responsibilities and incentive to manage efficiently;

(iii) improve information so that the right people are provided with clear, up-to-date information;

(iv) improve advice, bringing it closer to the line managers; streamlined central financial departments should monitor spending overall.

5.26 There is evidence to suggest that some local authority museums are benefitting from the introduction of such changes. Portsmouth City Museums Service, for example, which comprises six public museums (the City Museum and Art Gallery; D-Day Museum; Southsea Castle; Eastney Engine House; Cumberland House Natural Science Museum; and the Charles Dickens Birthplace Museum) has recently altered its management structure so that the Keepers of specialist collections are also managers of individual site museums with control over discrete budgets. By creating individual cost centres, it is possible to 'buy' services both from the museum department's central services and from other departments within the local authority. The site manager is also responsible for purchasing services from outside contractors. The advantages of these arrangements are greater accountability and efficiency; the latter advantage springing to some extent from an enhanced sense of 'ownership' on the part of the site managers.

5.27   Flexible staffing arrangements are needed if museums are to operate more efficiently. Glasgow City Museums, for example, have recently created a large pool of museum assistants from staff who previously had specific jobs concerned with security, cleaning and shop duties. Training is provided so that all museum assistants have the opportunity to develop a full range of skills, with the emphasis on customer care. The more skills individuals have, the more they earn, and there is enough money in the budget to allow for all museum assistants to reach the top of the grading system. The Director of Glasgow City Museums was quoted in the *Museums Journal* (July 1990) as saying that he would like to go further and 'achieve one scale, going right through to the curatorial, technical and conservation staff to give more movement'. The Director of Carlisle Museum has recently outlined a similar approach in *Museum Development* (October 1990) to appoint exclusively salaried staff to the new museum. 'There will be no distinctions made between staff in terms of staffroom facilities, training or representation. The intention is to arrive at staff integration and collaboration, with everyone trained in the principles of customer relations, requirements and every aspect of the visitor experience'. This move towards flexible staffing arrangements also facilitates the creation of project teams. In short, the aims and objectives of the museum should provide the touchstone for any decision about staffing.

5.28   The effective management of volunteers is also an issue which needs to be addressed. The Office of Arts and Libraries recently commissioned research in this area from the Ironbridge Institute and the University of Birmingham. The resulting publication *Volunteers in Museums and Heritage Organisations* provides guidance on 'best practice' relating to volunteer activity. It stresses, for example, the need to produce a policy towards volunteers which should involve consultation with all interested parties. The Museums Association's policy statement on volunteers in museums emphasises that 'volunteers can only in exceptional cases replace the trained, qualified permanent staff in the museum', and that the value of volunteers is in a supplementary and supportive role. It is important therefore that each museum should decide which areas of work are appropriate for volunteers and to provide the necessary resources for them to operate effectively. Volunteers need to be supervised. A volunteer co-ordinator, either on a paid or an unpaid basis, can increase the acceptability of volunteers among paid staff and ensure the smooth running of a volunteer programme. Museums should also consider creating a loose-leaf manual to include details about recruitment, induction and training procedures, and information on such matters as insurance cover, the payment of expenses, and Codes of Practice on Health and Safety. This approach will assist the integration of volunteers within the management framework of the museum as a whole.

Training Initiatives

5.29 The quality of a museum service depends heavily on a well-managed and skilled workforce. The MGC's report *Museum Professional Training and Career Structure* (1987) recommended that training should be available to all categories of museum staff throughout their careers in accordance with the needs of the employer and the individual. As a first step we RECOMMEND that all museums should regularly analyse the training needs of their staff in the context of the museum's forward plan. The Museum Training Institute (MTI) and AMC Training Officers can advise and assist in this area. They can also advise on the next step, which is to identify appropriate training courses which will meet the museum's priority needs.

5.30 One of the problems at the moment is the absence of a national structure for museum training. However, from 1991 the MTI will be acting as the Industry Training Organisation (ITO) for the museum industry, responsible both for setting and implementing training standards. At present, occupational standards are being established for all aspects of museum work – a system which will be linked with that of the National Vocational Qualifications (NVQs) administered by the National Council for Vocational Qualifications. In Scotland there will be Scottish Vocational Qualifications (SVQs) administered by the Scottish Vocational Education Council (SCOTVEC). This will make it easier to identify and prioritise training needs. It will also make it easier to choose training courses, since one of MTI's roles will be the accreditation of both training and training providers. We welcome the activities of the MTI, and we commend the decision of the Office of Arts and Libraries to provide revenue funding for the MTI in recognition of its national role in promoting museum training standards. We

RECOMMEND that local authority museum staff play their part in helping the MTI to develop standards, for example by participating in MTI's functional analysis groups.

5.31 In order to take advantage of the available training opportunities it is important that the resource implications are fully understood, both in terms of money and, where necessary, staff cover. We RECOMMEND that all museums should produce staff training policies and set aside at least 2% of the staffing budget for training and educational activity. We commend the *Charter for Staff Training* adopted by Leicestershire County Council for its Museums, Arts and Records Service in 1990. The provision of training, re-training and general educational development opportunities is declared to be a high priority for *all* staff of the Department. The new training strategy will encourage and support not just traditional areas of professional skills training but also, for example, attendant and technician training programmes; training in personal and management skills; relevant general education; attendance at professional meetings, conferences, and seminars with a training/staff development content; and study visits, secondments and attachments both within the UK and abroad. By 1992–93 it will be possible for all full-time staff to be released from normal duties for an average of a minimum of two working weeks per employee per year, (with pro-rata provision for part-time staff), for both formal and informal training. In return for their own training opportunities, wherever practicable staff will be expected to provide necessary professional or technical 'cover' – normally without additional payment – for colleagues taking advantage of the increased opportunities offered by the training Charter. A new post of Voluntary Work and Training Administrator has been created, partly to administer and promote the Leicestershire training programme and training opportunities.

5.32 We are particularly concerned that managers of museums should be able to receive appropriate training in order to meet the challenges presented by a rapidly changing local authority environment. With financial support from the MGC, the MTI is currently piloting a series of workshops including marketing for management; managing creativity; and leadership in museums. These themes were developed from a national training needs analysis funded by the MGC and carried out in 1988. We look forward to the development of a comprehensive management training programme, which takes full advantage of existing, reputable training providers. In this connection we welcome the

66

Business in the Arts management training bursaries scheme currently sponsored by English Estates, the MGC and the Arts Council. This scheme makes it possible for a limited number of senior arts and museums managers to attend short management courses at leading business schools at highly subsidised rates. Several local authority museums managers have won bursaries and we hope that there will be further initiatives of this kind.

6. Funding Considerations

Local Authority Revenue Expenditure

6.1   Income in support of revenue expenditure by local authorities in England is provided from revenue support grant, the national non-domestic rate, the community charge and other grants, fees and charges. The level of additional central support each charging authority receives in the form of Revenue Support Grant is determined by its Standard Spending Assessment (SSA). This represents the Government's assessment of the appropriate amount of revenue expenditure by each local authority taking account of its physical, demographic and social characteristics, consistent with the provision of a standard level of service, and the Government's view of an appropriate amount of revenue expenditure for all local authorities.

6.2   Provision for museums and art galleries is included in the District level All Other Services SSA. This covers all services provided by Shire Districts such as recreation, refuse collection, cemeteries and crematoria and the administration of housing benefit. It is calculated for all authorities which provide these services; that is Shire Districts, London Boroughs and Metropolitan Boroughs. The All Other Services SSA formula is primarily based on resident population adjusted to take account of the additional costs associated with commuting and tourism. About 70% of the SSA is distributed on the basis of this indicator. The remaining 30% is distributed by factors which evidence has shown are associated with higher costs – population density, population sparsity, social conditions and earnings levels.

6.3   It is not possible to identify a specific amount within the All Other Services SSA, either in total or for an individual authority, for any service element, such as museums and galleries, neither is Revenue Support Grant hypothecated to specific services. For the financial year 1991–92 the two main charges in the All Other Services SSA are an increase in the total to be distributed of over 28% and a doubling of the weight given to the tourism factor in the assessment formula. The latter change will benefit resorts and other authorities with large numbers of visitors. It will be up to managers of museums in these authorities to make the case for an appropriate increase in revenue funding on the basis that they are providing a valuable service for visitors to the area.

6.4   As a non-statutory service, museums are in a tough situation when competing for resources. What guidance can we provide concerning an appropriate level of local authority expenditure on museums? First, in reviewing museums' plans and setting levels of revenue funding we RECOMMEND that local authorities should take account of the MGC Registration Guidelines and the Museums Association's *Code of Practice for Museum Authorities* (1987), (see Appendix E). Due account should also be taken of the MGC's care of collection guidelines which are in course of preparation. Second, we repeat the RECOMMENDATION in the MGC report *Museums in Scotland* (1986) – the Miles Report – that a local authority museum should have separate access to its own accommodation, including stores, even in the smallest institutions, at least two curatorial staff with technical and attendant support and separately identified budgets for acquisition, documentation, conservation, display and ancillary activities. Advice on the appropriate level of service provision to meet an authority's particular situation can be obtained from Area Museum Councils. If an in-depth report is required, grant-aid towards the cost may be available.

6.5   Instead of directly operating a museum, an authority may wish to ensure that there is an appropriate level of museum provision in its area, by offering financial assistance to independent and/or university museums. In these circumstances we RECOMMEND that the local authority grant to such museums should bear comparison with the cost of directly providing a museum as set out in broad terms at 6.4.

Government Grants and Assistance available to Museums

6.6   AREA MUSEUM COUNCILS receive the largest proportion of their money from central government, in England through the MGC. Their members (including local authority museums) are able to obtain grants towards a wide range of museum activities on a project basis. The terms of reference for English AMCs are set out in the MGC's *Guidelines for Area Museum Council Grants to Clients*. The AMCs in Scotland and Wales operate under a broadly similar regime. Eligible schemes include the following aspects of museum work: conservation, storage, documentation, security, exhibitions, education, public services, technical services, photography, publications, marketing and training. 'Pump-priming' grants can be provided towards the employment of museum staff (especially curators, conservators and documentation specialists) but grants are not available for a museum's general running costs. AMCs can be flexible in the amount of money they give to members' projects so long as the grants do not exceed 50% of the total cost of all schemes assisted in any one year.

6.7   Each AMC sets its own priorities and issues a grant-aid policy annually. The Scottish Museums Council (SMC) policy for 1991–92 is exemplary in placing grant-aid within the context of museum planning. It states that the SMC will continue to place the highest priority on projects which are presented within the context of agreed and clearly defined development or management plans. It specifies that the plans should cover collections management, interpretation and education, research, marketing, financial planning, staff training and future developments. After the first phase of the MGC's Registration Scheme is completed in Scotland (1992) eligibility for project grant-aid will be dependent upon an approved plan being in place. The priority areas for project grant-aid for 1991–92 are divided into two groups. The 'key priorities' are management, marketing, fund-raising, conservation and collections management, industrial collections and natural science collections. 'Other priorities' are touring exhibitions, interpretation and education. The policy also states that while remedial conservation should continue to receive high priority, grants will be conditional upon future display and/or storage arrangements having adequate environmental conditions and security.

6.8   To some extent, SMC's policy reflects the priorities of its sponsor department, the Scottish Education Department. The English AMCs are given a freer hand to reflect the priorities of their members so long as they work within the MGC guidelines referred to at 6.6. It is interesting to note, therefore, that the English AMCs tend to give a lower priority to marketing and fund-raising than the SMC. There are signs that this situation is beginning to change, especially since grant-aid for management and marketing projects has been available direct from the MGC, but many museums have pressing needs relating to the documentation, conservation and security of their collections which AMCs must respond to with only limited funds at their disposal. The opportunities for museums to obtain external funding towards care of collection projects from business sponsors and educational charities are limited, so the AMCs play a vital role in supporting this area of activity.

6.9   The MGC's *Review of Area Museum Councils and Services* (1984) made a strong case for doubling, in real terms, the government grant to AMCs over a five year period to 1990. Little impact was made on this target, and we have no hesitation in RECOMMENDING that AMCs should have their current level of funding doubled by 1995. In England this would mean an increase from £2.84m (1990–91) to £5.68m (1995–96). We welcome the fact that the Office of Arts and Libraries (OAL) has begun to recognise the need and the MGC has been able to pass on an increase in funding to English AMCs in the financial year 1991–92 averaging 15%.

6.10   With improved levels of funding, AMCs will be in a better position to assist museums in tackling backlogs of documentation work which have been identified through the Registration process. They will also be more able to help museums tackle backlogs of conservation work identified by recent surveys such as *The Conservation of Industrial Collections* (1989), and *A Conservation Survey of Museum Collections in Scotland* (1989). There is a particular need to invest in preventative conservation through creating the proper environment for the display and storage of collections. These are obvious priorities, but many museums need assistance in other areas of work. For example, major local authority museums with important collections should be able to receive research grants for scholarly work on their collections leading to appropriate publications and exhibitions. At present, AMC grants of this nature are virtually non-existent.

6.11   Grants towards the purchase of exhibits are available through two complementary schemes which apply to both England and Wales, and a single scheme for Scotland which nevertheless covers much the same ground. The MGC *Purchase Grant Fund for the Regions*, administered by the V&A Museum, contributes towards the purchase of objects relating to the arts, literature and history by appropriate institutions in England and Wales. Grants towards the preservation in the public domain of items or collections important for the history and development of technology and science in all their branches can be obtained through the MGC's *Preservation of Industrial and Scientific Material (PRISM) Grant Fund*, which is administered on the MGC's behalf by the Science Museum. The PRISM fund is not restricted solely to the purchase of items because it is recognised that a significant part of the cost of acquisition often relates to transportation and conservation. The maximum grant that can be awarded through the purchase grant schemes is 50% and, in order to qualify for a full 50% grant, at least 25% of the cost must be found from locally raised sources, such as the applicant's own purchase vote, special appeals, contributions by Friends organisations, private donations from individual bene-factors or sponsorship. All applications are judged against the museum's published collecting policy.

6.12 The substantial increase in prices for many categories of material means that a local authority museum often finds it extremely difficult to finance a major purchase. Assistance from the purchase grant funds is therefore of increasing importance. However, the fact that they were 'frozen' almost throughout the 1980s means that they are now under severe pressure to respond effectively to demand. For example, the V&A's allocation of grant is limited to a maximum of £60,000 per institution annually while the PRISM fund has had to set a similar ceiling of £10,000. Without these restrictions the funds would be exhausted well before the end of each financial year.

6.13 The MGC has consistently argued for an increase in the purchase funds available to non-national museums and galleries. In the MGC's Annual Report for 1989–90 we were able to record our pleasure and gratitude at the Government's decision to increase the level of funding from 1990–91. Over the next two years the MGC purchase grant funds will rise by £468,000 to £1.75m; a modest increase in terms of the rise in art prices, but it will be welcomed by the hundreds of museums which benefit from these grants. We RECOMMEND that there should be regular increases in the purchase grant funds to take into account the real increase in prices of works of art and other categories of material over the last ten years.

6.14 In recent years, the NATIONAL HERITAGE MEMORIAL FUND (NHMF) has acted as a sort of 'backstop' for the regional purchase fund schemes in so far as applications have conformed with its own criteria. This situation has in turn, put a great deal of pressure on the NHMF. Many local authority museums have cause to be grateful to the NHMF and we welcome the fact that the Office of Arts and Libraries allocation to the fund is to rise from £1.5m in 1990–91 to £5.5m in 1991–92. However, the planning figures for the following two years show no increase in the allocation. We trust that this situation will be kept under review.

6.15 Some 70% of local authority museums are located in 'listed' historic buildings. As a result their capital requirements are often considerable. This burden falls principally upon local authorities but the impact of the community charge and government restrictions on capital borrowing are already having a serious affect on capital programmes. The availability of grant-aid from outside sources such as the Historic Buildings and Monuments Commission, the MGC, SMC and Council of Museums in Wales (CMW) can, however, provide a key to unlock funds. The MGC's CAPITAL GRANTS SCHEME has been particularly successful in supporting projects in England which involve the housing of collections in secure and environmentally controlled conditions. Another priority has been the provision of conservation workshop and laboratory space. Capital grants to local authorities act as a 'seal of approval' for museum projects, and in the past they have exerted a leverage out of all proportion to the actual size of the grants, which have often been derisory. Given the pressure on local authority budgets mentioned above, the need to increase the MGC's capital grant budget is becoming urgent if the scheme is to remain credible. At present, the fund averages £300,000 annually for the whole of England – a sum that could be swallowed up with ease by a single project. We RECOMMEND that the Office of Arts and Libraries should provide sufficient resources so that the MGC's Capital Grants fund can be increased to £1m by 1995. Commensurate increases in funding should be made available to the SMC and CMW who are empowered to assist capital development in their areas. In December 1990 the OAL announced that it was to sponsor a review of the building renovation needs of the National Museums and Galleries. We RECOMMEND that the OAL provides additional money to the MGC so that a complementary survey of the needs of non-national museums can be undertaken.

6.16   The lack of funding available to the capital grants scheme has meant that resources have had to be concentrated on care of collection projects. Schemes concerned principally with improvement to the presentation of the collections have attracted a lower priority. We welcome, therefore, the advent of the MUSEUM IMPROVEMENT FUND (MIF) which will be available initially for a three year period commencing in 1991. The MIF is funded jointly by the Wolfson Charities and the Office of Arts and Libraries, and money has been set aside for non-national museums throughout the UK. The grants are directed chiefly towards the internal refurbishment of museum and gallery display spaces, and it is possible to receive up to two-thirds of the eligible costs of a scheme. The MIF does not compensate however, for the recent demise of English Tourist Board (ETB) 'Section 4' grants which were able to assist the development of a museum's public facilities. The grants not only supported many new museum displays, but also assisted the provision of facilities such as public car parks and toilets designed to accommodate wheelchair users. The loss of 'Section 4' grants in England makes it even more imperative that the capital grants fund should be increased and that the MIF should continue for as long as possible.

6.17   The MIF is available to museums throughout the UK but we have noted that there are variations in the funding arrangements for England, Wales and Scotland for AMC, purchase and capital grants. A lacuna in grant-aid provision exists for Northern Ireland. We have already mentioned the emergence of the Northern Ireland Museums Advisory Committee (NIMAC) as a potential AMC, and we RECOMMEND that at the earliest opportunity, NIMAC should be given responsibility for administering government grants to non-national museums in the Province on the pattern of the SMC and CNW . We further RECOMMEND that the Northern Ireland Department of Education should provide sufficient resources to permit the extension of MGC's purchase grant schemes to local museums in Northern Ireland.

6.18   The Arts Councils often assist museums, even though their remit is not concerned directly with museums. Their concern with promoting the arts has meant that they work with organisations which share their objectives, and museums with a particular interest in contemporary art have benefitted from financial and other assistance. An important avenue of support for local authority galleries in recent years has been the Arts Council of Great Britain through its *Glory of the Garden* ART DEVELOPMENT STRATEGY (ADS). Over the first five years (1985–90) of the ADS, £2.5m of new funds have been allocated by the Arts Council. They have been matched by a total of approximately £3.5m from local authorities in three, four and five year agreements. This combined total of £6m may be the largest single injection of revenue funds to local authority museums and galleries in this period.

6.19   The Art Development Strategy aimed to achieve four things:

(i) To restore contemporary art to its rightful place within the country's art galleries.

(ii) In consultation and partnership with local authorities to help public galleries, throughout strategic areas, to develop their facilities and exploit their expertise and resources to maximum benefit.

74

(iii) Increased expenditure on schemes which encourage patronage of individual artists.

(iv) Continuation of the Arts Council's programme of regional touring exhibitions at the Hayward Gallery and Serpentine Gallery.

6.20 The ADS has been a success in far more than financial terms. In reviewing the achievements of local authority museums through the ADS a number of points should be highlighted. First, there have been significant increases in the origination of high quality exhibitions of national and international importance by regional museums, and the creation of touring exhibitions that challenge the traditional London focus for such tours. Second, there have been key developments in promoting black artists and the work of women artists; extensions in innovative exhibition making, cross-media collaborations and the presentation of performance art. Third, the debate about 'public art' has been heightened, providing a stimulus for public commissions and projects, and extending the role of the museum beyond its immediate walls. Fourth, there has been a significant development of visual arts education work in museums, culminating in the creation of the National Association for Gallery Education. Fifth, there has been an increase in the creation of thematic displays and exhibitions that explore the connections between historic artifacts and the work of contemporary visual artists. Finally, the profile of local authority galleries has been raised in the context of urban renewal and cultural development.

6.21 The Arts Council has been sensitive to the charge that it might be diverting resources away from permanent collections. It has been careful to prevent this. In all cases the local authority submission has had to demonstrate that curatorial posts were filled first, that support services would not be jeopardised, and indeed, more positively, that there would be proper co-operation between keeper staff working on fine and decorative arts collections, and those staff working on exhibitions, education and community outreach. In only one museum, Manchester City Art Gallery, have there been major cuts that have threatened the validity of the partnership. In two cases, Preston and Nottingham, part of the ADS funds were spent, in collaboration with the Contemporary Art Society, on new acquisitions for permanent collections.

6.22 The Art Development Strategy will continue for another five years (1990–95) but on a financially declining basis. It is hoped, therefore, that local authorities will progressively make up the funding from their own resources and that the achievements of the ADS will be further developed in future.

6.23   The Arts Council has rightly stressed the important issue of making museums and galleries and their collections more accessible. We share their interest in generating more travelling exhibitions. The MGC's *Grants for Travelling Exhibitions Scheme* has had a modest success in stimulating touring, especially between local authority museums. However, the budget is tiny in relation to the need. To support travelling exhibitions in 1990–91, the MGC dispenses grant-aid which is equivalent to one-tenth of what, in today's money, the V&A's Circulation Department cost in its final year. The normal range of grants, between £1,000 and £10,000 is too small to make a significant contribution to touring by the national museums which, as far as OAL was concerned, was the main reason for its funding. Equally the budget is too small to halt the decline in touring by the Area Museum Councils, and this was not, in any case, part of its original purpose. The scheme has been most successful in assisting touring by the middle range of museums, especially in the form of cost-sharing collaborations between museums of similar size and resources. Museums administered by local authorities have been the main users of the grants scheme, since they tend to be multi-disciplinary, and have maintained programmes of exhibitions even though the sources have tended to dry up. There is no doubt that money has been siphoned out of touring, most noticeably – but not exclusively – by the closure of the V&A Circulation Department. The MGC is currently preparing a 'National Plan for Touring' which will attempt to quantify how much is missing from the touring economy, and how any new resources might best be deployed.

6.24   The MGC is also concerned about access to museums and galleries by people with disabilities, and is preparing a Code of Practice relating to museums and disability issues. This will propose that all museums should adopt disability policy statements and action plans, and maintain a regular dialogue with disabled groups. We welcome the creation of the ADAPT FUND which is designed to assist primary arts venues including museums to provide essential adaptations and facilities which benefit people with disabilities. The fund was established in November 1989 by the Carnegie UK Trust with support from the Office of Arts and Libraries and some fifteen museums and galleries (over half of them operated by local authorities) had benefitted by grants amounting to over £100,000 by September 1990. Grants are available at up to 50% of the costs, subject to a maximum of some £25,000.

6.25　The government's allocation to the BUSINESS SPONSORSHIP INCENTIVE SCHEME (BSIS) is set at £3.5m for 1990–91 and the three successive financial years. The BSIS is administered on behalf of the Minister for the Arts by the Association for Business Sponsorship of the Arts (ABSA) and since its inception in 1984 many local authority museums and their sponsors have benefitted from awards. The scheme is intended as an incentive to a business either to sponsor the arts for the first time or to increase its commitment to the arts. First time sponsorship may be matched £1 for £1 by the government, while additional sponsorship from a business that has sponsored the arts before (but not for more than three years) may be matched on a £1 to £4 basis. Organisations are eligible for two awards each financial year up to a maximum of £25,000.

6.26　Eligible activities for BSIS include, but are not limited to, commissions, productions, tours, festivals, concerts, exhibitions, buildings and refurbishment, and purchase of equipment. The financial award received by the arts organisation is intended to be used in some part to enhance the sponsorship. This may include extra advertising of the sponsored event, offering the sponsor an extra event either free or at a special rate, or the extension of a tour to further venues, for example, thus ensuring increased benefits for the sponsor. It will be clear from the above, that the scheme is not a top-up for an arts organisation but, as its title implies, an incentive to a business. It is in addition an incentive to, and a tool for, an arts organisation to seek sponsorship.

6.27　ABSA would be the first to point out that sponsorship should not be seen as an alternative to the core funding of museums by local authorities. Most of the BSIS awards to local authority museums have gone towards temporary exhibitions and special events such as concerts. This by no means diminishes their importance both in cash terms and as a signal to local authority committees that their museums service is sufficiently enterprising to gain external recognition of this kind. Useful advice on how to obtain business sponsorship is to be found in the ABSA/W H Smith *Sponsorship Manual*.

6.28　Sponsorship in museums involves ethical issues. Rule 6.2 of the Museums Association's *Code of Conduct for Museum Curators*

(1987) states that 'in the area of industrial sponsorship there will be an agreed relationship between the museum and the sponsor, and a curator must ensure that the standards and objectives of the museum are not compromised by such a relationship'. There is also a supplementary guideline which points out that 'commercial sponsorship may of itself involve ethical problems in respect of the products or political connections of the intending sponsor. Although there clearly has to be a trade-off between sponsor and museums, so that the former obtains promotional benefits in return for the financial support given to the museum, great care must be taken that an acceptable balance is struck. Displays, catalogues and promotional material may otherwise appear to be merely the vehicle for the sponsor's own promotion'. Rule 5.5 of the Code is also relevant here because it clearly states that 'museum objects on public display, with all forms of accompanying information, should present a clear, accurate and balanced exposition and must never deliberately mislead'. It goes on to say that 'these principles apply also to books and information published or otherwise disseminated by the museum'.

6.29   We endorse the Museums Association's Code of Conduct rules concerning business sponsorship. We also note that ABSA is conscious of the need to promote a proper understanding between sponsors and arts organisations, and we welcome their recent publication titled *Principles for good practice in arts sponsorship* (1990).

6.30   In recent years, museums have been able to benefit from various Manpower Services Commission (MSC), and now Training Agency, schemes. The MSC Community Programme for example, was used extensively in connection with museum documentation, interpretation, and general refurbishment projects. The replacement of the Community Programme by the EMPLOYMENT TRAINING (ET) SCHEME has resulted in fewer people being employed on museum schemes. However, we understand that the new Training and Enterprise Councils may be able to introduce greater flexibility to ET at a local level and museums may be among those to benefit. It is important that the lessons learned from past experience are taken into account. If museums are to be involved in government training schemes we RECOMMEND that adequate resources should be made available, particularly through the employment of appropriate specialists as supervisors.

6.31   The Training Agency is one of a number of government agencies which offer support to museums from time to time but whose agenda is not concerned with museums *per se*. The Miles Report (1986) noted that a number of government funded agencies in Scotland provided support to museums, including the Countryside Commission for Scotland, the Scottish Tourist Board (STB), the Scottish Development Agency (SDA), and the Highlands and Islands Development Board. The Miles Report called for better co-ordination of effort. It also pointed out that a lot of the money coming from government agencies related to capital projects and there was a real concern about the future viability of some newly established museums. We are pleased to record that since 1986 there has been an encouraging degree of co-operation between the Scottish Museums Council and such agencies as the STB and the SDA. Effective co-operation and liaison at national level is vital in order to ensure value for money and cost-effectiveness in new museum developments. If the museums are not established on a sound basis the problems will almost certainly end up with the local authorities.

6.32   Some evidence we have received criticises the sheer diversity of funds which museums have to tap in order to provide a proper level of public service. Much staff time is taken up by fund-raising at the expense of basic museum work. It has been suggested to us that central government funding should be radically altered – core funding for museums being met through a per capita level of funding allocated to museums via the MGC and AMCs working in close co-operation with local authorities. We do not consider this approach to be appropriate, bearing in mind the diversity of provision throughout the UK and our rejection of the idea that local authorities should have a mandatory duty to provide museums. We do believe, however, that there should be a greater effort to co-ordinate the central government funding available to museums. Several grant schemes launched by the OAL for example, in recent years, would have operated more smoothly and beneficially for museums if the MGC and AMCs had been consulted more fully and at an earlier stage.

Admission Charges and Earned Income

6.33   The *Public Libraries and Museums Act* (1964) permits local authorities to make a charge for admission, taking into account a museum's educational role. The *Museums UK* survey revealed that 30% of local authority museums charged for admission compared (at that date) to 38% of national and 69% of non-publicly funded museums. The MGC has endorsed the Museums Association's policy on admission charges (see Appendix F). In essence, the policy asserts that there should be a presumption against charging by local authorities. However, the decision whether or not to charge should be separately considered for each individual museum bearing in mind its location, the appeal of its collections, the impact of charging on its public and its financial situation. If a charge is imposed the museum should benefit from the additional income; concessions should be made to appropriate categories of visitor; and there should be free access to all visitors for one day per week or equivalent. Charging for temporary exhibitions is a separate and generally less contentious issue.

6.34   The City of Carlisle's Tullie House Museum and Art Gallery is currently undergoing a complete transformation at a cost of some £5m to the local authority. In order to fund the 400% increase in museum staff, the Council has decided to introduce a charge for admission. However, Tullie House will become a 'part-charging' institution which only levies a charge on the Border Galleries upstairs and not for instance, on the exhibition galleries on the first floor which inverts the usual rule-of-thumb of free access to collections and admission charges for temporary exhibitions. This inversion reflects not only the increase in staff and the cost of the new building, but also the fact that the main displays are targeted at the tourist market and are expected to change more regularly than the usual 'permanent' displays. The changing programme in the temporary exhibitions gallery is aimed largely at the local population, as a way of maintaining interest in the museum, as well as introducing contemporary art to north Cumbria as part of the Arts Council's Gallery Development Strategy. Furthermore, there will be no charge for local residents who will be identified by a 'Tullie Card' available at a cost of 40p. While Carlisle are about to introduce admission charges others are removing them. The City of Birmingham abolished charges at its branch museums in 1985 and attendance figures rose by an average of 126% in the first year following abolition. As we have said, a local authority must make up its mind about admission charges according to the particular circumstances of each of its museums, but many of those who gave evidence to our working party strongly support the notion that there should be a presumption against charging on the basis that museums are fundamentally an educational service and are not profit-led.

6.35   As an alternative to admission charges some museums might be tempted to consider a structured system of voluntary donations.

We believe that the setting up of such systems should be subject to the Museums Association policy mentioned above. Many museums already provide a donation box for visitors' contributions and we RECOMMEND that the proceeds should be used for the benefit of the museums service. With regard to the question of charging for enquiries, it is our view that as a fundamental part of its duties of public service, a museum should not levy charges for research carried out in response to enquiries made by individual members of the public. Neither should charges be levied as between one museum and another; museums are all stewards of the nation's heritage and it is a responsibility held collectively. The decision as to whether or not to charge for research conducted on behalf of a commercial organisation should be determined by individual museums.

6.36   There is a wide range of commercial opportunities available to local authority museums and any income generated from these activities should be retained by the local authority museum to enhance the service. Commercial operations should always be carefully considered in the context of the museum's mission statement and marketing plan, and there should be no illusions about the amount of money which might be made. There is no doubt that a good local authority MUSEUM SHOP *can* make money, but turnover should not be confused with profit. Furthermore, to work out the true net income, a museum should take into account such factors as the cost of staff dealing with sales and the notional rental cost of the floor space occupied by the shop. It is worth considering the possibility of contracting out the shop operation. Birmingham have done this successfully. In the final analysis it may be decided that a museum should operate a shop primarily because of its educational and public relations value rather than its commercial return. It is interesting to note that 79% of museums have a shop or sales point (1987) and more than half of museum visitors use these facilities.

6.37   In addition to shop trading there are many other ways in which a local authority museum can generate income. They include, for example:

(1) CATERING: though not usually a great money-spinner, is often seen as an indispensible service. Local authority museum catering is subject to compulsory competitive tendering.

(2) LICENSING: this has been developed at several local authority museums including Brighton and Temple Newsam House, Leeds. The latter benefitted by tens of thousands of pounds from an

arrangement whereby historic wallpapers found there were reproduced by Messrs Zoffany. In return, a number of museum rooms were wallpapered, free of charge, by the manufacturer with replicas of the original papers.

(3) MUSEUM EVENTS: these might include conferences, seminars, craft fairs, and concerts.

(4) HIRE OF FACILITIES: these might include the hire of appropriate museum spaces for everything from business meetings to weddings. Careful consideration needs to be given to the conservation and security implications of these arrangements.

(5) SPECIAL EXHIBITIONS: some local authority museums such as Edinburgh City Museums and the Yorkshire Museum have generated significant amounts of income from major exhibitions in recent years. In the case of the Yorkshire Museum, the local authority (North Yorkshire County Council) has created a special rolling fund for temporary exhibitions. All the proceeds from the exhibitions are fed back into this fund to finance the future programme.

6.38   Trading by local authority museums can be problematic due to the extensive and complex financial regulations governing local authority activities. It may be appropriate to use the model provided by the Passmore Edwards Museum (London Borough of Newham) which has established a Charitable Trust together with an associated trading company limited by guarantee. Existing museum shop stock was handed over to the trading company as a loan and it was agreed that the value of stock was to be repaid to the Borough over a three year period. If a museum has no stock then the local authority may need to consider a grant or loan for the initial purchase of stock. At the Passmore Edwards Museum, the trading company, after all charges have been met, covenants its surplus to the Trust to be used in accordance with the aims and objects of the charity. Any local authority museum which has serious intentions of achieving a reasonable return through its commercial activities must consider the appointment of a commercial manager.

Private Sources of Assistance to Museums

6.39   We have already referred to the important role of business sponsorship for the arts, and there are many charitable organisations which regularly provide grant assistance to local authority museums. This is not the place for a detailed guide to fund-raising, but we would like to pay particular tribute to the work of the National Art Collections Fund which has helped so many local authority museums to acquire important works of art for their collections. And we should also draw attention to the splendid work of 'Friends' organisations both in terms of their fund-raising activities and their general support for local authority museums. A new publication titled *Tax Effective Giving to the Arts and Museums: A Guide to Fundraisers*, published by the MGC and the Arts Council may prove very useful to those charitable Friends organisations which are actively engaged in fund-raising for local authority museums.

7. Recent Government Legislation affecting Museums

The Education Reform Act 1988 (England and Wales)

7.1   The rich variety of museum resources has made an important contribution to pupils' education for many years, through exhibitions, school loans and museum based activities. Museum education services now have a new prominence because of the emphasis on learning from original sources, as upheld by the introduction of General Certificate of Secondary Education (GCSE) course work and examinations, and more recently by the National Curriculum which is being phased into all State maintained schools in England and Wales and is designed to give every child from 5 to 16 a broadly based education. Comparable arrangements are being introduced in Scotland and Northern Ireland.

7.2   While new and exciting collaborations between museums and schools are already beginning to evolve, there are, however, aspects of the Education Reform Act which appear to threaten the very existence of some museums' education services. The implications of the current legislative changes in education and the effect on museums can be divided into three sections.

NATIONAL CURRICULUM

7.3   In recent years many schools and museums have co-operated in establishing programmes of work for GCSE pupils in addition to the successful work already done with younger pupils. Building on this experience, museum education staff and teachers in schools will need to assess the opportunities for integrating the learning potential in museums into the programmes of study in all curriculum areas. Local Education Authorities (LEAs) and schools are working to establish the new arrangements through local courses for teachers, school governors and staff, with these courses being funded by central government. We RECOMMEND that museums and museum educators should look carefully at all the core and foundation subject Statutory Orders and non-statutory guidance for each subject as they are published, to see how they can most usefully provide a related study programme. They should then establish links with LEAs and schools to promote appropriate in-service training courses.

7.4   In order to assist museums' understanding of potential links between their collections and the National Curriculum, the NCC has recently produced a helpful publication titled *The National Curriculum: A Guide for Staff of Museums, Galleries, Historic Houses and Sites* (1990). Other government-funded publications which provide useful case studies include *Museums and the Curriculum* (1988); *Arts and Schools* (1990); and *Initiatives in Museum Education* (1989). These publications have been distributed widely and are a welcome recognition of the vast potential that museums have to offer in the context of the new National Curriculum. They reinforce the findings of a whole series of recent HMI Reports concerning the educational value of museums.

7.5   In response to the challenge presented by the National Curriculum, some museums are jointly marketing their resources to schools. With financial assistance from the MGC/OAL marketing budget, museums in Hertfordshire are producing an education pack in the form of a loose-leaf binder, containing a list of all museums within the county with their subject biases, together with notes on topics which link directly to the National Curriculum. Other inserts will be added in phases as the Statutory Orders are published. On the history side, for example, museums are cross referenced to projects which include: 'The Way We Live', 'The Romans in Britain' and 'Researching Your Past.' These are linked to statutory and proposed attainment targets and programmes of study, and recommendations are made to encourage cross-curricular links. The *Museum File* will shortly be available to all schools within Hertfordshire and copies may be purchased by outside organisations. We RECOMMEND that other museums should collaborate in this way and we further RECOMMEND that Local Education Authorities, whether or not they fund museum services, should provide financial support towards such initiatives. Additional money from the Department of Education and Science (DES) and/or Office of Arts and Libraries (OAL) may be necessary for this to be a realistic proposition.

7.6   It is important that museums and schools recognise the widest possible range of education opportunities offered by museum collections. The HMI Report *A Survey of the Use Schools Make of Museums Across the Curriculum* (1989) showed that pupils' interest and understanding of the many areas of the curriculum had been enhanced by visiting museums and using objects in the classroom. In particular, work in language development, science, history, art and craft, design and technology was improved by first hand experience of museum collections. However, the HMI recommended that teachers, advisers, and museums could consider how work in other areas of the curriculum such as mathematics and geography could benefit from museum visits. Birmingham Museum has recently grasped this nettle and offered a series of activities with a mathematical theme. Pupils in the 7–9 age group visiting the museum were put in the role of a scientist using their own measurements to try to discover how fast Tyrannosaurus Rex could run. In the Art Gallery, 12–16 year olds explored 17th Century landscape paintings from a mathematical point of view, examining the artists' use of perspective to create the effect of distance and constructing their own 3-D card landscape reliefs. Meanwhile younger children at the Nature Centre looked at 'Animal Coats', finding out about adaptation to climate and habitat and constructing tally charts, bar graphs and set circles. We commend this imaginative approach.

7.7   While it is obviously important for museums to do all they can to help schools gain an understanding of their resources, it is also vital for teachers to receive training in the effective use of these resources. We have already mentioned the desirability of museums getting involved with in-service teacher training courses. However, we are also concerned that the initial training of teachers should alert all students to the educational potential of museums across the National Curriculum. We welcome the fact that some one-year Postgraduate Certificate in Education (PGCE) courses do incorporate study programmes designed to focus on learning from museum resources. We understand that some Bachelor of Education (BEd) undergraduate courses also include similar studies. Examples of current practice were outlined in *A Survey of the use of Museums in Primary Phase Courses in Initial Teacher Training* (DES 1990). However, with the advent of the National Curriculum and its implications for the use of museum resources we RECOMMEND that the DES guidelines for the training of teachers at BEd and PGCE level should be revised to specify the practical study of learning from museum resources as a mandatory part of initial training. This would consolidate guidance issued in DES Circular 24/89 which states that 'students should be aware of the range of agencies and other facilities with which schools co-operate including social services . . . and museums'.

LOCAL MANAGEMENT OF SCHOOLS (LMS)

7.8   From 1 April 1990, the management of secondary school and larger primary school budgets began to be delegated by LEAs to individual schools, thereby drastically reducing the role of LEAs in determining how money is spent. There are two categories of central services excepted from delegation to schools – mandatory and discretionary exceptions. Some of the discretionary exceptions, including museum education services are currently subject to an overall 10% limit in relation to the general schools budget.

7.9   At the present time, approximately half the LEAs in England wholly or partly fund museum education services. If museum education is retained by an LEA, its funding is likely to come under increasing pressure. It is worth remembering however, that County Councils have the power to grant-aid museums, such expenditure being charged to general funds unless it is explicitly conditional on the provision of education services. Only in this latter case is it a charge on the education budget. If museum education is not included within an LEA's discretionary budget, a museum will have to charge schools individually for its services and thus become one of the many areas of expenditure subject to local determination by school management. Access to museum resources may not be regarded as a priority by a school's governing body and as a result may not receive financial support.

7.10   From 1 April 1991, Kent County Council (KCC) museum education service (renamed The Outreach Collection) will be part of a new Client Services group within the Arts and Libraries Department. The museums service will be located within the Heritage Group. The Outreach Officer has conducted a survey of his potential 'clients'. It appears that schools are aware of the educational value of museum objects. They value the items provided by the Outreach Collection, particularly because the Collection can make available items which it would not be practicable to purchase from departmental resources and because it can offer large loans of associated items which it would be impossible for teachers to obtain in any other way. However, the survey showed that an alarming number of headteachers had compartmentalised the service as 'something to do with the history department', and were genuinely amazed at the potential for such subjects as science, art and English which the Outreach Collection can fulfil.

7.11 Clearly, the Kent survey has been useful as a marketing tool but when the crunch comes it is still unsure how many schools will take up the offer and whether they are prepared to pay. It is expected that, as part of an income generation requirement, a standard loan will cost £15 and a large loan £50. Previously there were no charges. The Outreach Collection will be available to groups and organisations in addition to KCC educational bodies. Arrangements concerning the Collection's acquisition and disposal policy in relation to that of the museums service and the provision of adequate storage conditions and administrative support are still under discussion. Uncertainties of the kind facing the Outreach Collection affect other museum education services and we are extremely concerned that a number will close and then become very difficult or impossible to revive. The DES and LEAs should recognise both the value and vulnerability of museum education services. We RECOMMEND that museum education services should normally be funded by the LEA from its discretionary budget and provided with at least the present level of resources.

CHARGES FOR SCHOOL VISITS

7.12 The Education Reform Act upholds the principle of free education established in the 1944 Education Act. Under the principles set out in DES circular 2/89, schools may not charge for activities necessary to fulfil the requirements of the National Curriculum, or for those that take place wholly or partly during the school day. Parental contributions towards the cost of a school visit must be voluntary and no pupil whose parents are unable or unwilling to contribute should be excluded from a visit. Schools must find supplementary funds (eg from the School Fund) for visits if parental contributions do not cover the costs. This was made clear in a recent DES decision to turn down a bid from an LEA, as part of its submission for LMS, to hold back part of its schools budget for a central fund to subsidise visits for children from low income families. Any money earmarked for such hardship cases should now be delegated to schools through funding formulas.

7.13 Although the basic legislation on school charges for visits has not changed since 1944, confusing advice on its interpretation has caused great uncertainty in the teaching profession. A survey by the Group for Education in Museums (GEM) in 1988–89 indicated that this uncertainty had an adverse effect on most of the museums which responded. However, there are signs that school visits to museums are beginning to pick up again. Indeed, some museums saw an increase in school visits during 1989–90. From the evidence to date, we can draw some preliminary conclusions as follows:

(i) There is a new emphasis by schools on the quality of a museum visit and, in particular, its relevance to the National Curriculum.

(ii) There seems to be a decline in the number of recreational day trips, often arranged at the end of term, which may no longer be considered as educationally valid if they are not directly related to curriculum studies, and therefore not justifying the request for parental contributions.

(iii) Staffing problems in schools can occasionally lead to the last minute cancellation of museum visits. Problems include covering for staff absences, non-availability of supply teachers and the pressure on teachers trying to cope with the new demands of curriculum and assessment arrangements. The Yorkshire Mining Museum experienced a 29% fall in school visits in the summer months of 1989 and had to bear the costs of extra casual staff who would have dealt with large pre-booked school parties who made last minute cancellations. Lack of staff cover seems to be a particular problem for secondary schools when contemplating visits to museums.

(iv) There is concern that schools with a high proportion of pupils from low-income families might have experienced difficulty in obtaining sufficient parental contributions to pay for school visits.

(v) Museums which rely heavily on admission charges and income from cafeteria and shop sales for revenue suffered considerable financial losses in 1989, and concern has been expressed by some small independent museums about their future commercial via-bility. Many already operate discount schemes for school parties either by offering a free visit for every tenth child in a group, or by offering an annual membership scheme in which schools are allowed an unlimited number of visits on payment of a subscrip-tion. Incentive schemes will no doubt be increasingly introduced if falling visitor figures continue.

(vi) In some cases there has been an increased demand for museum education staff to visit schools, as a consequence of difficulties in funding school trips, and also sometimes of teachers' unwillingness to assume the legal responsibility for their pupils on excursions out of the classroom. This situation also highlights the increased importance of school loan services operated by museums. However, as we have already seen, the advent of LMS is placing the future of a number of loan services in jeopardy.

7.14 It is very clear that under the Education Reform Act governors of schools will have an important role to play in curriculum and financial policy decisions. Teachers will have to display clear aims and objectives by establishing the study visit's credibility in educational terms if they are to gain financial support from the governors of their schools. This means that the teacher will have to be familiar with the museum and to have negotiated a programme of study with the museum staff. To help create the right climate of opinion among school governors the MGC and GEM have recently circulated a leaflet to every maintained school in the country. This leaflet is aimed specifically at school governors and spells out the educational opportunities presented by museums, especially in the context of the National Curriculum.

Museum Education Policies

7.15 The educational purpose of museums needs to be explicit in their corporate strategies. We RECOMMEND that all museums should produce education policies based on guidelines which the Group for Education in Museums is currently formulating. These policies should take into account the contribution which museums can make to learning about ethnic and cultural diversity. Useful case studies can be found in the HMI Report *A Survey of the Use Schools Make of Museums for Learning about Ethnic and Cultural Diversity* (1988), while the Geffrye Museum and the ILEA have published a report titled *Black Contribution to History* (1988) which recommends ways in which the museum should strive to move away from its Eurocentric approach. Museum education policies also need to address provision for all visitors with special educational needs. Valuable information and advice on this subject can be found in the HMI Report *A Survey of the Use Some Pupils and Students with Special Educational Needs Make of Museums and Historic Buildings* (1987), and in Anne Pearson's article about museum education and disability – published in *Initiatives in Museum Education* (1988).

7.16 Of course it is one thing for a museum to produce a museum education policy: implementation is another matter altogether. In the MGC report *Museums in Scotland* (1986) it was stated that 'if museums are to realise their full potential as educational instruments, museum education must be treated as a specialised activity calling for museum education officers. They will have had training as teachers or communicators and their functions should be to assist curators and other museum staff in making the most effective

90

presentation and interpretation of museum collections, and to maintain communication between the museum and a broad and varied audience both within and beyond the local community. A museum education officer should also take responsibility for museum-based programmes within the community and act as the prime agent in the use of the museum by schools, colleges and other education organisations and special groups'. We have no hesitation in endorsing the RECOMMENDATION that where possible museums should have specialist education staff, and if lack of funds precludes this, the possibility of a number of museums sharing an education officer should be explored. In either event we RECOMMEND that local authorities should give favourable consideration to the funding of such posts.

7.17   So far as Area Museum Councils (AMCs) are concerned, they are able to grant-aid one-off educational projects undertaken by their member museums. We RECOMMEND that all AMCs should develop policies towards education, not only in respect of grants towards projects of a specifically educational nature, but also taking into account such matters as the educational potential of display schemes which they support. We commend the Area Museums Service for South Eastern England's insistence that grant-aid for a display project will be contingent upon advice being received from a conservator and an education specialist.

7.18   Finally, there is the question of national co-ordination relating to museums and education. Within the DES there is an HMI with responsibility for evaluating the use of museums as an educational resource. The Arts Council employs an officer with a specific brief to develop education in galleries and exhibition spaces in England particularly in relation to contemporary visual arts. Museums lack anyone with comparable responsibilities and we RECOMMEND that the MGC gives consideration to the appointment of a full-time museum education adviser. Additional funds would be required to create such a post.

The Local Government Finance Act, 1988 (England and Wales)

COMMUNITY CHARGE

7.19   The Local Government Finance Act has led to the introduction of the community charge and the Uniform Business Rate to replace the rating system in England and Wales. Scotland has a similar system which was introduced a year earlier. In September 1990 the MGC commissioned a survey by Peat Marwick McLintock (Management Consultants) to investigate the impact of the community charge on museums funded by local authorities. It was not possible to undertake any quantitative analysis because the community charge is too newly introduced to be able to identify any meaningful trends or statistics. However, the survey identified a number of areas of concern.

7.20   From a sample of 32 local authorities, 10 reported that the change in the rating system has made little difference to their operation. For those with operational problems it was difficult in some cases to isolate the community charge as the cause. Non-payment of the community charge was a concern for several authorities and was not restricted to any particular type of authority. It was anticipated that current levels of non-payment could lead to cash shortages later during the financial year 1990–91, and would create budget shortages in future years. There was little evidence of museum services being singled out for greater cuts than other areas of local government expenditure. However, because curators are often only able to control a small part of their budgets (because of 'fixed' staffing and premises costs), any reductions in, or restrictions on, expenditure affect these 'variable' costs disproportionately. Furthermore, the policies and practices of an authority can constrain the way in which curators are able to respond to changes. For example, a 'no-redundancy' policy will limit the options available for instituting savings.

7.21   So far as local authority museums are concerned, financial pressures are affecting the collections management process in a number of ways. Curators are having to take on additional responsibilities as posts are frozen and new needs arise, purchase funds are sometimes frozen, while building closures and failure to provide on-going operational funding can lead to degradation of collections. In addition, Derbyshire County Council's proposed sale of part of their museum's collection in order to generate cash for general expenditure could have serious repercussions for all local authority museums. Financial pressures are also affecting public services. Closure of out-stations and reduced opening hours have occurred, while the freezing of posts has led to cuts in specialist services, such as education. At Bristol, for example, the City Council's Museum Service may have to close all its branch museums in 1991–92 while its education service is also under threat. The business rate for Bristol Museums and Art Gallery is some £180,000 in 1990–91. It is our view that local authority museums should not have the business rate deducted from their budgets so as to place vital areas of museum activity at risk.

7.22 There is also an impact on the general management of museums. The problem of 'fixed' costs in relation to museum budgets has already been mentioned. As a result, where cuts in expenditure are required, they tend to be concentrated in the areas of the budget where costs are controllable, such as exhibition displays, marketing or promotion. The speed of change facing local authority managers has made it very difficult for proper planning processes to be instituted, and few curators have been equipped with appropriate management skills to tackle these issues. This has been further heightened by the practice of introducing mid-year cuts.

7.23 Looking to the longer term, the full effect of non-payment will only emerge over a period of years. In addition to causing short-term problems in the financial year 1990–91, non-payment may have the effect of forcing community charge levels up in the future, to compensate for those who are not paying, and at the same time making those who do pay more vociferous about how their money is to be spent. One-off cuts in expenditure, for example, the freezing of posts, may cause temporary concern but will not necessarily affect the long term development of a service. However, there is a danger that the continual erosion of budgets over a number of years will lead to a permanent decline in the standard of service offered. As this report was being completed we were learning of alarming threats of further cuts to many museums in 1991–92 following the government's announcement of standard spending assessments to local authorities.

7.24 In order to deal with the changes brought about in part by the introduction of community charge and the Uniform Business Rate, curators and managers will need to develop new skills and ways of operating. The Peat Marwick Survey concluded that this process could be assisted by the following:

– greater delegation of financial responsibility so that curators are able to manage a greater part of their budgets;

– management development initiatives to increase the planning and strategic and financial management skills of curators;

– pump-prime funding to enable income generating projects to develop without requiring an immediate return.

We endorse these conclusions.

7.25   Independent museums are generally benefitting under the new Uniform Business Rate with many of them now eligible for an 80% reduction where previously they only received a 50% reduction on the old rate. Grant assistance from local authorities to independent and university museums does not generally appear to have been affected at present, but discretionary grants are clearly going to come under increasing scrutiny in the future. Indeed, the community charge and the close proximity to capping for Cheshire County Council means that it is likely to cut its contributions to independent museums in the county. The annual contribution to the Norton Priory Museum Trust, for example, is likely to be reduced by £20,000 (from a current budget of £129,000) over the next four years. Another example is the Manchester Jewish Museum which had its revenue grant of £3,120 from Oldham cut in March 1990 as a result of severe financial constraints exacerbated by the introduction of the community charge.

COMPULSORY COMPETITIVE TENDERING

7.26   The introduction of compulsory competitive tendering (CCT) needs to be seen in the context of the Government's clearly-stated ambition to turn local authorities from being direct providers of local services to being purchasers or facilitators of services provided by others. *The Local Government Finance Act* (1988) requires competitive tendering for refuse collection, street cleaning, catering, cleaning of buildings, grounds maintenance, vehicle maintenance, and anything else named in future by the Secretary of State for the Environment – at present only sports and leisure facility management. If a local authority wishes to carry out the work by its own directly employed labour, then it must win the right to do so by bidding successfully against private sector companies. It must not do anything which would 'restrict, distort or prevent competition'. While an authority need not accept the lowest tender it would need a good reason for not doing so. If an authority does win the right to do the work by direct labour it must keep a separate trading account for each of the defined services. Furthermore, these services must make a surplus sufficient to make a specified rate of return on capital and no cross-subsidisation between trading accounts is allowed.

7.27   It is clear that CCT will have a profound effect on all aspects of local authority work. For example, the need to ensure that Direct Labour Organisations (DLOs) can be effective in competition against the private sector will lead increasingly to a closer examination of central service costs. Service departments such as museums pay for the services they receive from personnel, finance, law, computers and other central departments through the central establishment charge. Henceforward, central departments will have to operate in effect on a trading basis, stating clearly what services they are offering, quoting unit prices for them, and allowing the client department more choice in the level of central services that they use. Museums should no longer accept the imposition of a central establishment charge without questioning how the total cost was arrived at.

7.28   So far, however, the direct impact of CCT on museums has not been great because few if any of the activities specified for CCT affect their primary functions. For example, relatively few local authority museums operate their own vehicles, let alone have the luxury of a vehicle maintenance section within their own department. So far as catering is concerned, local authority museums have been rather behind independent museums in providing appropriate services and in any case they have often been contracted out to private businesses. The maintenance of grounds is usually only marginal to the interest of museums, and in any event local authorities can exempt from their CCT contracts grounds maintenance and horticultural work in botanic gardens, including those with an historic orientation, open to the public.

7.29   The introduction of CCT in relation to the cleaning of buildings can present more of a problem for museums where separate cleaning staff are now used, especially as the museum must pay any extra supervision costs, which in turn probably cannot be offset against the contract. However, in recent years many museums have reorganised their attendant and cleaning workforces so that attendant staff typically do most or all of the routine cleaning between the start of their work period and the actual opening of the museum to the public. In such arrangements, the cleaning activity per employee is likely to average well below the CCT cut-off point of 50% of their working time, and hence that part of the council's work would not have to go out to tender.

7.30   As mentioned, the Secretary of State has the power to add other local authority services to the CCT list by Parliamentary Order. There is some concern that security might be added to the list with unfortunate consequences for museums. It should be recognised that museums have special security needs. This is due in part to the nature of museum collections and exhibitions but a major factor which must be taken into consideration is the public relations role of warders/attendants. Attendants who identify with their museums and over whom museum management has direct control are more knowledgeable, better able to handle questions and more attuned to their public relations role. It is no accident that vocational qualifications for museum attendants have been offered by the Museums Association for many years, and are currently being further considered by the Museum Training Institute. The general problem with private security guards is a lack of continuity both because contractors tend to shift personnel from one site to another as deemed necessary and as a result of a high turnover of staff. Rapid turnover makes the in-house training of attendants difficult, if not impossible. There is also a managerial problem arising from the mixed loyalties of contract security guards. Security contractors will usually have no experience of museum security and the museum must therefore provide most of the training. For most museums this would require a full-time security coordinator to act as liaison with the contractor. Confusion can quickly arise as the security guards begin to receive instructions from two directions. We therefore RECOMMEND that routine museum security should be an in-service provision, and if security is added to the CCT list museum security should be exempted.

7.31   There may, of course, be situations where the use of commercial security firms would be appropriate, for example in coping with special events when additional manpower is required to supplement the museum's own security force. They can also serve when additional after-hours protection is needed in specific high-risk situations. Further advice on the use of private security contractors can be obtained from the MGC's Museums Security Adviser, and we commend the Museums Association's *Guidelines on Security when using Outside Contractors*. Useful information about museum security generally is to be found in *Security for Museums* (1990) by Nell Hoare.

7.32   At the present time CCT is almost exclusively concerned with 'blue collar' work, but it would be wrong to think that professional services and activities will be unaffected by the new climate. In cases where museums form a small part of a Leisure Services Department, it is possible that the contracting out to private concerns of major Departmental activities will lead to a shrinkage of support services, such as finance and personnel, which are currently available to museums. Furthermore, the Audit Commission is encouraging local authorities to be fully aware of their own performance in professional areas such as museums. The comparative efficiency of in-house services in professional areas where there is an 'outside' market is bound to come under increasing scrutiny. Obvious areas of activity for such scrutiny are design and exhibition production and at least some areas of conservation work. Many local authority museums of course, already contract out design and conservation work on a project-by-project basis. The maintenance of museum standards is obviously of vital importance, and recent initiatives such as the MGC's Register of Conservators will help to overcome legitimate concerns. In general it should be acknowledged that the provision of a wide range of services on a competitive basis is not new to museums. A large capital project, for example, will involve the competitive selection of architects, designers, and other specialists; tendering by construction companies; and the supply of goods and services, including maintenance, on the basis of competitive quotations. The application of competitive tendering to a complete museum service, however, is another matter altogether, and it should be remembered that local authorities already have the power to follow this course if they so wish.

7.33 We understand that at least two local authorities have recently been through the exercise of requesting their museum curators to draw up tender specifications for the museums service but have not taken the matter further. At Poole, however, in 1988 there was a competitive tendering process for a significant portion of the museums service, namely the new Waterfront Museum. The idea that the Waterfront Museum should be subject to competitive tendering was not part of the original plan. It was a direct response to rapidly escalating project costs which caused local authority members to question whether officials had got their sums right. The best way to test whether the museum had estimated the remaining costs accurately was by seeking tenders from the private sector. The preparation of the brief was the responsibility of an official in Poole's finance department who received professional advice from museum staff. An advertisement in the national press invited tenders for designing, setting up and managing the Waterfront Museum and some 25 companies responded – a mixture of mainly heritage, leisure and attraction operators. In the final analysis only four tenders were received including one from Poole Museum.

7.34 Poole Museum's tender set out four main objectives for the Waterfront Museum: to provide a resource centre for the museum's education service; to provide an attractive range of displays with a quality retail outlet; to provide refreshment facilities for visitors; and to provide full accommodation for the professional and technical services of Poole's museums. The museum's professional input to the tender document was complemented by a market strategy provided by the Tourism Service and a financial appraisal drawn up by a member of staff (working on a confidential basis) within Poole's Treasurer's Department.

7.35 The museum's bid was unashamedly set in the context of the museums service's requirements as a whole. On the museum's projections the Council was to provide an annual contribution of £55,000 a year for the first five years whereas some of the other tenders had offered substantial income to the Council immediately and a guaranteed income in subsequent years. Poole Council decided in favour of its own museums service having come to the conclusion that museological as well as financial criteria needed to be taken into account.

7.36 The attitude of Poole Council is interesting in the light of the Museums Association's recently declared policy on 'privatisation' This states that 'Most core functions of museums, such as the care of collections, scholarship and educational services can never be provided at a good professional standard on commercial criteria alone'. The policy also states that 'The guardianship role of the local authority with respect to the collections they hold on behalf of the public should be regarded as inalienable. Therefore ownership of the collections must remain in the public domain irrespective of whether the museum is administered in future in the public or private sector'. However, the Museums Association's policy statement also recommends that local authority museums should adopt an increasingly business-like approach to the provision of services. It recommends that cost-centre analysis of the existing or future service should be undertaken to identify those elements in the museums service which could be managed on the basis of partial or complete cost recovery. It further recommends that vigorous and enterprising business systems should be considered (either in-house or external) to ensure the maximum income generation consistent with giving value for money from non-core elements in the service such as sales points, publications and catering.

7.37 We call for the improved planning and evaluation of museum operations to be based on agreed standards of collection care, and to take place within a framework of responsible trusteeship. Otherwise there is a very real danger that local authorities will not be able to distinguish the demands of economy from those of efficiency and effectiveness. Some standards already exist, for example in the form of the MGC's Registration Scheme guidelines. Others are currently being produced, for example the MGC's forthcoming series of care of collection standards relating to different types of museum collection. It is important that these are put in place as soon as possible so that any ideas to introduce competitive tendering for core elements of a museums service can be debated on the basis of agreed museological criteria as well as financial considerations. And it will be important for the Museums Training Institute to consider what training is required to equip relevant museum staff with the skills to deal with competitive tendering.

Local Government and Housing Act 1989 (England and Wales)

7.38 Part V of the Act regulates local authority interests in companies. Museums which fall into the local authority 'controlled' category, regardless of whether they have charitable status or not, will be subject to the full range of controls. Local authority 'influenced' companies are also subject to the full range of controls unless they fall into an exempt category. One such exempt category covers companies set up solely for charitable purposes. So, although the majority of museums are local authority 'influenced' companies, they usually have charitable company status and will thus be exempt from the legislation. It is important to note that four conditions must be satisfied in order to fall into this exempt category, as follows:

(i) the company must be set up solely for charitable purposes;

(ii) fewer than half of the company's directors may be associated with one local authority;

(iii) the local authority must declare that the company operates independently of the local authority;

(iv) the local authority must declare that, in settling the terms of any transaction with the company, they have not taken into account any future borrowing or capital expenditure proposed by the company.

7.39 Some confusion has been caused by the fourth condition. The DoE advise that the question of the new capital finance system for local authorities is concerned only with capital borrowing and credit arrangements. It no longer bites on local authority capital expenditure. Thus, if a local authority wishes to give a capital grant to a museum it does not count against any sort of limit. However, if the local authority or a company which it influences or controls wishes to borrow money to finance a development, that would count against the local authority's borrowing limit unless the company was in an exempt category. As the assumption seems to be that most local authority influenced museum companies fall into the charitable exemption category, the DoE believe this should not be a problem.

7.40 Section 13 of the Act brings into question the voting rights of Friends of Museums and similar organisations of local authority museum committees. Advice from the DoE is that general exemption from the provisions of Section 13 is given in Regulations 4(1)(a) and 5(2)(c) of the Local Government (Committees and Political Groups) Regulations 1990. The effect of these Regulations is to maintain the voting rights of co-opted members of committees and sub-committees established exclusively for the management of land and buildings owned or occupied by a local authority. The exemption therefore permits users or experts, such as Friends of Museums, to be co-opted, provided that the committees or sub-committees are responsible for the management of museums, but not for setting the budget. Using another Regulation, 5(2)(e), the Hastings and St Leonards Museum Committee and Yorkshire Museum have received exemption from Section 13.

7.41 In general terms this is a classic example of legislation affecting museums by default (the Education Reform Act is another example). At the heart of the problem is the fact that museums are not a mandatory local authority service. We are not recommending a change in this position but this does mean that the OAL, (as the government department responsible for museums) the MGC and the MA must remain vigilant in assessing the impact on museums of proposed legislation.

8. The Economic and Social Importance of Museums

The Economic Importance of Museums

8.1 Since the publication of John Myerscough's report, *The Economic Importance of the Arts in Britain* (1988) the particular contribution of museums to the economy has been better understood. The report revealed that museums were a buoyant sector with a turnover which amounted to £230m. It emphasises the fact that a significant area in which museums contribute to the economy is that of employment. Not only do jobs exist in museums, previously unemployed people have been able to find permanent jobs via the short-term government-funded projects in which many museums have participated. Outside museums, the provision of goods and services required by museums and their visitors have resulted in employment within the local community. Myerscough reported that the impact of museums in this field was greater than other cultural activities. Museums are also of direct benefit to arts and crafts since they not only buy works of art but employ artists for educational purposes and often sell their work in museum shops. The job-creating potential of museums in areas of high unemployment is also in tune with the tourist 'honey-pots'.

8.2 The provision of special exhibition programmes can attract significant numbers of visitors with a resulting impact on the local economy. An extremely successful instance was the 'Gold of the Pharaohs' exhibition presented by Edinburgh City Council in 1988. It was calculated that the exhibition generated £5.5m expenditure in Scotland, of which £4.4m was spent in the city itself.

8.3 Many towns and cities now realise the benefits which flow from drawing up arts policies, especially if the local authority aims to attract new businesses to the area with a view to regeneration. Myerscough's report noted that senior executives are placing increasing value on cultural amenities as a means of encouraging the economy, a means of improvement and of sustaining confidence in an area. It was also felt that the cultural facilities indicated 'a dynamic, self-confident host community.' Businesses also found that such cultural provision, in which museums played a role, made re-location more acceptable to staff and was useful in their recruitment. Newport Borough Council's Economic Development Unit has frequently used Tredegar House (part of the local authority museums service) on its promotional literature. This has undoubtedly been a factor in the successful establishment of a business park adjacent to Tredegar House and its attractive grounds.

8.4 The contribution of museums to the economy, as well as their educational and cultural role, has been recognised by government-sponsored agencies which support museums. An analysis of the position was given in the MGC report *Museums in Scotland* (1986). Five agencies, including the Scottish Tourist Board (STB) and the Scottish Development Agency (SDA), were examined which together spent considerably more on museums than the Scottish Museums Council (SMC). The report recommended that circulars should be issued to government agencies indicating that they should not support the establishment of new museum-related developments unless the SMC and the relevant local authority or authorities agreed that the project concerned was sound and well thought out in museum terms and likely to be financially viable in the long run. We have already noted that the liaison between SMC and agencies, such as the STB and SDA, has improved in recent years.

8.5 Central government funds (through the OAL) have supported the establishment of the National Museum of Photography, Film and Television in Bradford and the Tate Gallery, Liverpool, both of which have played an important role in re-inforcing the cultural amenities of cities which recognise the importance of such facilities in regenerating their economies.

8.6 The Yorkshire Mining Museum (YMM), an independent museum with good links with Wakefield Council, has benefitted by support from the Council's Economic Development Unit which regards the YMM as an asset in the drive to increase tourism and promote the area as a place for business relocation. The Museum has received derelict land grants and an EEC grant of £510,000 as it was regarded as being of benefit to surrounding Assisted Areas. Urban Development Corporations have also assisted museums as part of urban regeneration programmes. The North Woolwich Old Station Museum in London's Docklands which opened in 1984 was created by the Passmore Edwards Museum Trust, with capital funding from the London Dockland Development Corporation, while the Merseyside Maritime Museum received assistance from the Merseyside Development Corporation.

8.7   The myriad of grants available through many different central government and EEC agencies to assist in urban regeneration schemes has had a scattered impact on museums perhaps because museums were not envisaged as direct beneficiaries. In the last decade, local authority and other investment in museums has been found in such cities as Glasgow, Hull and Birmingham. This support has provided, or is about to provide, cultural facilities which evidence shows will be in the forefront of broader-based regeneration programmes to take the cities into the next century. We RECOMMEND that local authorities who create regeneration policies take into account the role of their museums or museums which they support.

Museums and Tourism

8.8   It could be said that museums and tourism have always co-existed. As far as local authority museums are concerned, however, a more formal relationship has grown in certain parts of the UK with the establishment of the Tourist Boards and the adoption by some authorities of a tourism strategy. The Miles Report examined in detail the relationship between the Scottish Tourist Board and museums.

8.9   The evidence presented to the Working Party suggested that most museums are keen to be associated with tourism as a means of encouraging a wider range of visitors. It is accepted that 'tourist' does not merely refer to visitors from overseas but those spending at least one night in an area and those 'day visitors' who come from outside the vicinity. Even in so-called 'non-tourist' areas, there will be visits to friends and family which would potentially include trips to a museum. The importance of tourism to the economy is now well understood. UK domestic tourism (excluding day visits) earned £10.765m in 1989 while the value of overseas tourist spending in the same year was £8.502m. Given this background, it is noteworthy that 27% of overseas tourism business is inspired and motivated by museums, galleries and the theatre.

8.10   We have already expressed our regret that 'Section 4' Tourist Board grants, which aided the installation of visitor facilities in museums, were withdrawn from England. We welcome the fact that the grants continue to be available in Scotland and Wales, although we note with regret that the Northern Ireland Tourist Board cannot support museums.

8.11   Given the tremendous and sustained popularity of museums, the amount of productive liaison between tourist boards and museums varies greatly in different parts of the UK. A recent initiative in the North West Museum Service area saw museums and the North West Tourist Board together promoting 'Heritage on your Doorstep'; a scheme to increase awareness of what museums have to offer and to encourage visits. The MGC also supported this scheme through its management and marketing initiatives fund. The Lincolnshire County Museums Service had benefitted from the County Council restructuring in 1984 which placed museums and tourism together within a Recreational Services Department. Applications for English Tourist Board (ETB) grants were successful and the Service has also gained access to professional designers financed by the tourism section as well as using the tourism budget to produce publicity leaflets. In certain cases, a fruitful relationship has been developed by siting Tourist Information Centres (TIC) within museum premises. The Willis Museum, Basingstoke and the Westbury Manor Museum, Fareham, both part of the Hampshire County Museums Service, are examples of this arrangement, while Newport Museum in Gwent has a TIC situated in the same area as its museum shop and reception area.

8.12   A dialogue between arts organisations, including museums, and the ETB began in 1990 with a view to establishing methods of promoting the arts more consistently within a tourism context. We applaud and encourage this initiative at national level. We RECOMMEND that museums also continue to forge links with local Tourist Boards and Tourist Information Centres, and we RECOMMEND that there should be effective liaison between AMCs and Regional Tourist Boards, for example, through co-options to each other's Boards of Management. We also RECOMMEND that when local authorities create formal tourism strategies they take fully into account the role museums can play.

8.13   It is important, however, that the educational role of museums should not be submerged in the drive to increase tourism. As the negative environmental impact of tourism is better understood, museums should seize the opportunity to act as centres of debate on conversation related matters. Far too few museums actually place conservation issues before their visitors, whether it is the conservation of the built or natural environment within which they work, or the conservation of their own collections.

Museums in Urban Areas

8.14   Most urban museums were established by local authorities before the last War, and their collections tend to be very broadly based. The branches which may provide a museum presence throughout the wider urban area tend often to have a narrower scope. In recent years there has been a growing awareness that publicly-funded services should be truly available to and used by all sections of the community. Many museums have taken positive steps to inform those living in urban areas, which include inner cities and suburban estates, about what their museum has to offer and how they can become involved in its work.

8.15   Research projects to identify those not visiting museums, followed by outreach programmes and activities within the museum to encourage visits and involvement, have been success-fully undertaken in a number of museums, for example, at Manchester City Art Gallery, which began its research in 1986. As a result, the exhibitions programme now has objectives linked to the responses received during the research. A free Community Loan Exhibition scheme has established exhibitions on popular topics available to non-museum venues. The Gallery's mailing list was also expanded to include contacts made during the research, and a licensed cafe opened in the building.

8.16   Museum staff and collections have an important role to play in encouraging participation by all sections of the community. The appointment of staff with specific responsibilities in this area, such as the Ethnic Minority Co-ordinator in Glasgow Museum and Art Galleries, has resulted in new audiences being reached. Curators may be involved in this process by displaying existing collections which originated from around the world not merely as curiosities but as a means of exploring cultural diversity and revealing, for example, the technical skills of the makers and the social context within which the objects were produced. An interesting initiative in this field is Birmingham Museum's 'Gallery 33' which uses ethnographic and other collections to present a diversity of traditions and reference to ethnic groups within the Birmingham population.

8.17   Another approach, used, for example, at Leicestershire Museum, is to increase considerably the proportion of objects in certain fields. In the case of Leicestershire, the collection of Indian arts and crafts acquired by the Decorative Arts Department began with the 1975 Acquisitions Policy and expanded considerably in the 1980s (see 8.18). As we have already noted, the Geffrye Museum in Hackney has been reviewing its display policy and is seeking to move away from its traditional 'Eurocentric' approach. As a result of being attracted to museums by such initiatives visitors will, it is hoped, be encouraged to discover other facets of the collections and museum activities.

8.18   Some local authority museums, including Leicestershire and Bradford, obtained funding under Section 11 of the *Local Government Act* (1966) in order to establish posts to improve links with ethnic communities. At Leicestershire Museums two posts were established in 1982, one being an Assistant Keeper for Indian Arts and Crafts while the other, a Teacher Leader (Multicultural Education) has countywide responsibility for introducing schools groups to specially developed collections which reflect the cultural diversity of the County. Section 11 funding originally covered 75% of the salary of an assistant keeper of ethnic collections at Bradford Art Galleries and museums. The post was later regraded to keeper level, the salary difference being found by the Council. A collection covering arts and social history of the Asian and other communities in Bradford is being formed and programmes of temporary exhibitions and outreach are in position. The recent suspension of this funding at a time when it was still needed has led to the call for its reinstatement by many organisations, including the Museums Association. We concur.

8.19   The emergence of community museums within urban areas has taken two forms. One has involved a planned strategy to involve local people more directly in the activities of local authority museums. A good example is Springburn Museum in Glasgow. The other has involved the setting up of new independent museums as a result of activity within the community. An example in an urban area is the Jewish Museum in Manchester which has received some local authority support since it was established in 1984. It has been suggested that local authorities should support such independent museums with professional guidance and financial assistance. It may be that beneficial effects to the community of the existence of a museum would justify special consideration when the level of support is being assessed. The importance of museums as institutions which give communities their 'roots' is particularly relevant in New Towns. The museum at Stevenage, for example, has been particularly successful as a focus for community activity.

8.20   Until recently, towns and cities in manufacturing areas hardly ever participated in tourism. Now, with the decline of industry, tourism and heritage have made a considerable impact on

many urban areas. Certain local authority museums have benefitted by receiving greatly needed capital investment, additions to
staff and finance for marketing initiatives. However, that curators'
perceptions of museums' cultural and educational contribution to a
tourism strategy are not immediately recognised by other Council
departments which are usually leading the project. Of prime
importance is the need to ensure that local people are also able to
benefit from and participate in improvements created with tourists
in mind.

Museums in Rural Areas

8.21 The number of rural museums has grown considerably in
recent years alongside the boom in tourism. Although most
museums in rural areas are independent, some are part of local
authority County services, such as those administered by Norfolk
and Leicestershire, and a significant number of District museums
are in rural localities. The collections are principally concerned
with the history of the immediate area, chiefly rural, local industries
and buildings. One exception is the Bowes Museum in County
Durham which has an internationally important fine and decorative art collection. There are also a small number of furnished
historic houses (owned by local authorities), such as Lotherton Hall
outside Leeds.

8.22 Evidence presented to the working party suggests that
museums in rural areas recognise their role as tourist attractions,
but also recognise a relationship with the local community. Such
museums can both preserve and explore the heritage of the area.
Many museums have also recognised that they form a focus for the
community to which they also give a sense of identity. This can
have a particular significance when rural communities are in a state
of flux due to movement into and out of the area. Arising from this
is another aspect of their role noted by museums in north east
Scotland: the increasing demand for information from people
researching into family history.

8.23 The organisation of very small scale touring exhibitions
from larger museums is an important method of supplementing
specialised collections, and of bringing fresh experiences to rural
areas where no museums exists. The Norfolk Museum Service has,
for example, organised two-case exhibitions intended for libraries.
It is clearly important that the security and environmental

conditions of the potential venues (which could include church halls or schools) are adequate for the type of exhibits which are to be displayed. The provision of such a service seems at the moment to be done on an *ad hoc* basis. We have already noted that the MGC is currently preparing a national plan for travelling exhibitions which will examine the overall provision of exhibitions in the UK.

8.24 A method which has successfully tackled some of the constraints of rural museums is the creation of active regional forums or countywide committees, which has led to joint initiatives with peripatetic curators, conservation, and loans. The work of the Borders Museum Forum in Scotland has been of particular significance in this regard.

8.25 Government agencies concerned with rural areas have occasionally supported museums. For example, museums such as Pendle Heritage Centre in Lancashire have benefitted from Countryside Commission grants. The designation of a part of Suffolk as a Rural Development Area has resulted in two museums being awarded grants from the Rural Development Commission. We welcome this involvement subject to there being proper consultation with AMCs and local authorities.

8.26 Grants to independent museums in rural areas are also provided by many local authorities, including those which are not themselves a museum authority. We should like to see such grants as part of a formal museums policy as mentioned elsewhere in this report. A welcome trend especially in Scotland, has followed the requirement for Scottish local authorities to provide adequate cultural provision. This has led to the employment of museum professionals to support the independent museums in their area within a formal policy. The very large number of museums in rural areas of Scotland have benefitted from this development. Similar arrangements, although non-statutory, have been established in certain Districts and Counties in England and Wales.

8.27 In areas with sparse cultural provision, museums can provide a useful means of breaking the isolation for those without access to transport in the cities and larger towns. The Arts Council's report *Think Rural: Act Now* (1989), although not specifically concerned with museums, contains details of many arts initiatives which have taken place in rural areas of relevance to museums.

8.28 As far as museums which are part of a larger service are concerned, the existence of a museum in a rural area may stimulate visits to other museums in the service as well as being a potential source for donations and information. However, their management is subject to particular constraints which arise from their situation. The museum, if part of a group, may be remote from the Service headquarters or may be suffering from underfunding and inadequate levels of staffing compared to the rest of the Service. As many such museums are open for only part of the year, the provision of adequate educational and visitor facilities may not be given a sufficiently high priority.

Future Opportunities

8.29   Evidence submitted to the Working Party confirms the existence of a growing awareness by local authorities that museums have a vital role to play in the social and economic development of their areas. With local authority and central government support, museums in all parts of the UK are contributing to the regeneration of the economy. Museums have been shown to be central to the growth of tourism and further initiatives in this field are anticipated. The widening of audiences in both urban and rural areas has been achieved by targetting specific groups, although much remains to be done, especially in rural areas. We believe the evidence suggests that the future holds considerable opportunities for museums to sustain and widen their contribution.

9. Summary of Conclusions and Recommendations

Chapter 1 – Introduction

1. A number of factors have affected the relationship between local authorities and museums during the past decade. Some of them have been 'external': for example, the abolition of the Metropolitan County Councils; changes to the education system brought about by new legislation, the introduction of the community charge and government restrictions on local authority capital borrowing and revenue expenditure (1.1). Other factors have been 'internal': for example, the introduction of the Museums and Galleries Commission Registration of Museums Scheme and the emergence of a new and comprehensive framework for museum training under the auspices of the Museum Training Institute. (1.2).

2. Local authorities may wish to support museums for a variety of reasons – educational, social, recreational and economic. Based on their collections, museums represent a unique cultural resource which is worthy of investment (1.3–1.7).

Chapter 2 – The Legal Framework

3. We recommend that all local authorities with museum powers should adopt policies to ensure an appropriate level of museum provision in their areas and that these policies should be reviewed regularly (2.7). We further recommend that the Office of Arts and Libraries and the Department of the Environment should issue a joint circular to local authorities to this effect. We also recommend that the relevant Government Departments in Scotland, Wales and Northern Ireland should follow suit (2.12).

4. We recommend that the following factors should be taken into account when a local authority assesses whether or not there is an appropriate level of provision in its area: a) the availability of museum collections relating to the historical, scientific and cultural heritage, and the natural environment of the area of benefit, b) the existence of MGC Registered or Provisionally Registered museums within the area, and c) the public availability of museum resources throughout the year (2.10).

5. We recommend that all museums operated by local authorities should seek Registration and that local authorities should consider Registration as a basic criterion when considering support for independent museums (2.11).

6. We recommend that the government should consider extending powers to operate museums to Parish, Town and Community Councils in England and Wales (2.13).

7. We recommend that local authorities operating museums should be more aware of their trustee role and of guidelines for their conduct in this role which include a strong presumption against the disposal of items in a museum's collections (2.16).

Chapter 3 – Local Authority Museums

8. We recommend that all local authorities should endorse the Museums Association's Guidelines for Museum Committee Members (3.8).

9. We recommend that all local authority museums should employ professionally qualified and/or experienced curators in line with the MGC Registration guidelines (3.9).

10. We recommend that local authorities should regard separate departmental status for the museums service and chief officer status for the director as the preferred option when considering their organisational arrangements (3.16). However, we recognise that a number of museums services have flourished within larger departments, such as leisure (3.17).

11. We recommend that a local authority should only consider transferring its museum operation to a charitable trust if it is doing so for positive reasons, such as the desire to take advantage of greater opportunities to raise money from private sources. Continued support of the museum's core activities may be needed if standards and service levels are to be sustained (3.21).

Chapter 4 – Local Authorities in Partnership

12. We support the concept of jointly operated local authority museums services, but there must be a strong commitment by all the partners if the maximum benefits are to be obtained (4.1–4.7).

13. We recommend that all local authorities with museum responsibilities should become members of Area Museum Councils (4.9).

14. We support the concept of museum networking as manifested in Area Museum Councils and Countywide Consultative Committees and Forums (4.8–4.15). We support further developments in respect of management consortia (4.16).

15. We recommend the establishment of the Northern Ireland Museums Advisory Committee (NIMAC) as a fully fledged Area Museum Council with appropriate government funding (4.19).

16. We recommend that all potential local authority nominated committee members of independent museums should be invited to indicate their willingness to be guided by the Museums Association's *Guidelines for Committee Members* and to acknowledge their corporate and personal liabilities under the museum's constitution before any offer of appointment is finalised (4.22).

17. We recommend that partnerships between local authorities and independent, armed services and university museums should be subject to written agreements (4.25).

18. We recommend that registered independent museums should be allowed to benefit from Private Treaty Sales in their own right (4.28).

19. We recommend that all charitable and non-profit distributing independent museums should be allowed the full 100% relief on the Uniform Business Rate (4.32).

20. We recommend that local authorities should continue to support armed services museums and seek ways to assist the preservation of publicly owned military collections which are currently without any professional oversight (4.39).

21. We recommend that local authorities should recognise university museums' contribution to the cultural and educational amenity by making an appropriate level of recurrent financial help available (4.48).

22. We recommend that all university museums should take steps to establish more formal lines of communication with the wider museum community (4.51).

23. We urge national museums not to charge fees in excess of costs reimbursement for loans to local authority museums (4.53).

24. We urge national museums to provide more touring exhibitions, and seek enhancement of the MGC's capital grants scheme to assist the provision of temporary exhibition areas (see also recommendation 38 (4.54).

Chapter 5 – Managing Museums – Recent Developments

25. We recommend that AMCs and Countywide Consultative Committees/Forums should work together to encourage collecting agreements between museums wherever appropriate (5.5).

26. We recommend that all museums should develop forward plans and utilise related performance indicators (5.19).

27. We recommend that all local authority museums should publish reports on a regular, and preferably annual, basis (5.20).

28. We recommend that wherever possible, local authority museums should employ designated marketing managers, possibly on a shared basis (5.22).

29. We recommend that AMCs should consider the appointment of marketing advisers on the pattern of the Scottish Museums Council (5.22).

30. We recommend that museums should collaborate on joint marketing initiatives and seek support from AMCs and Regional Tourist Boards (5.24).

31. We support the idea that museums should produce policies towards volunteers (5.28).

32. We recommend that all museums should regularly analyse the training needs of their staff in the context of the museum's forward plan (5.29).

33. We recommend that local authority museums play their part in helping the Museum Training Institute (MTI) to develop standards, for example, by participating in MTI's functional analysis groups (5.30).

34. We recommend that all museums should produce staff training policies and set aside at least 2% of the staffing budget for training and educational activity (5.31).

Chapter 6 – Funding Considerations

35. In reviewing museums' plans and setting levels of revenue funding we recommend that local authorities should take account of the MGC Registration Guidelines and the Museums Association's Code of Practice for Museum Authorities, 1987. We further recommend that a local authority museum should have separate access to its own accommodation including stores even in the

smallest institutions, at least two curatorial staff with technical and attendant support and separately identified budgets for acquisition, documentation, conservation display and ancillary activities (6.4).

36. We recommend that the local authority grant to independent and/or university museums should bear comparison with the cost of directly providing a museum if it is not already operating one (6.5).

37. We recommend that AMCs should have their current level of funding doubled by 1995 (6.9).

38. We recommend that there should be regular increases in the MGC's purchase grant funds to take into account the real increase in prices of works of art and other categories of material over the last ten years (6.13).

39. We recommend that the Office of Arts and Libraries (OAL) should provide sufficient resources so that the MGC's Capital Grants fund can be increased to £1m by 1995 (6.15). We recommend that the OAL should provide additional funds to the MGC so that a survey of the building renovation needs of non-national museums can be undertaken (6.15).

40. We recommend that NIMAC should be given responsibility for administering government grants to non-national museums in the Province on the pattern of the Scottish Museums Council and Council of Museums in Wales at the earliest opportunity (6.17).

41. We recommend that the Northern Ireland Education Department should provide sufficient resources to permit the extension of the MGC's purchase grant scheme to local museums in Northern Ireland (6.17).

42. We recommend that adequate resources should be made available, particularly through the employment of appropriate specialists as supervisors, if museums are to be involved in government training schemes (6.30).

43. We recommend that the proceeds from donation boxes for visitors' contributions should be used for the benefit of the museums service (6.35). There are a wide range of commercial opportunities available to local authority museums and any income generated by these activities should be retained by the museum (6.36).

Chapter 7 – Recent Government Legislation Affecting Museums

44. We recommend that museums and museum educators should look carefully at all the core and foundation subject Statutory Orders and non-statutory guidance for each National Curriculum subject as they are published, to see how they can most usefully provide a related study programme. (7.3).

45. We recommend that museums should collaborate in marketing their educational resources in the context of the National Curriculum and we further recommend that Local Education Authorities, whether or not they fund museums services, should provide financial support towards such initiatives (7.5).

46. We recommend that the DES guidelines for the training of teachers at BEd and PGCE level should be revised to specify the practical study of learning from museum resources as a mandatory part of initial training (7.7).

47. We recommend that museum education services should normally be funded by the LEA from its discretionary budget and provided with at least the present level of resources (7.11).

48. We recommend that all museums should produce education policies based on guidelines which the MGC and the Group for Education in Museums are currently formulating (7.15).

49. We recommend that where possible museums should have specialist education staff and, if lack of funds precludes this, the possibility of a number of museums sharing an education officer should be explored. We also recommend that local authorities should give favourable consideration to the funding of such posts (7.16).

50. We recommend that all AMCs should develop policies towards education, not only in respect of grants towards projects of a specifically educational nature, but also taking into account such matters as the educational potential of display schemes which they support (7.17).

51. We recommend that the MGC gives consideration to the appointment of a full-time museum education adviser (7.18).

52. In order to deal with the changes brought about in part by the introduction of community charge and the Uniform Business Rate, curators and managers will need to develop new skills and ways of operating (7.24).

53. We recommend that routine museum security should be an in-service provision and, if security is added to the compulsory competitive tendering list, museum security should be exempted (7.30).

Chapter 8 – The Economic and Social Importance of Museums

54. We recommend that local authorities which create urban regeneration policies take into account the role of their museums or museums which they support (8.7).

55. We recommend that museums continue to forge links with local Tourist Boards and Tourist Information Centres and we recommend that there should be effective liaison between AMCs and Regional Tourist Boards, for example, through co-options to each other's Boards of Management (8.12).

56. We recommend that when local authorities create formal tourism strategies they take fully into account the role museums can play (8.12).

Appendix A *Local authority net revenue expenditure on museums and galleries*

	1983–4	1984–5	1985–6	1986–7	1987–8
					£ millions
England (a)	57.3	62.6	68.6	67.5	76.0
Wales (a)	1.7	1.9	2.3	2.5	2.8
Scotland (b)	—	—	—	11.6	13.4
Northern Ireland (c)	—	—	0.5	0.5	0.6

Source:

(a) Actuals. Taken from *Local Government Financial Statistics, England and Wales* (HMSO) with additional information supplied by DoE and Welsh Office.

(b) Actuals. Taken from *Scottish Local Government Financial Statistics* (Scottish Office).

(c) PSI survey of Northern Ireland local authorities.

First published in Cultural Trends 1989:4 © Policy Studies Institute

Appendix B *Local authority capital expenditure on museums and galleries(a)*

					£ millions
	1983–4	1984–5	1985–6	1986–7	1987–8
England	14.7	20.3	21.1	13.8	13.0
Wales	0.7	0.6	0.6	0.5	1.4
Scotland	1.9	2.7	1.8	1.8	0.8

Source: Local Government Financial Statistics, England; DoE; Scottish Local Government Financial Statistics; Scottish Office; Welsh Office.

(a) Gross expenditure.

First published in Cultural Trends 1989:4 © Policy Studies Institute

Appendix C *Museums Association: Code of Practice for Museum Committee Members, Trustees and Members of Governing Bodies*

The Museum

1.1   All Committee members are private individuals who, together with their fellow members of the Governing Body, are trustees for the public, and have the premises, collections and resources in their Museum's care as assets in trust. Each is answerable for this duty to his or her own conscience and in the last resort to the courts, and not primarily to those responsible for their appointment to the Governing Body.

1.2   A Committee member should ensure that clear objectives and a development plan (whether known as such or as a corporate or business plan) for the institution, are both prepared and monitored, and should encourage the drafting and circulation of a museum policy manual based upon it.

1.3   As much as the Director/Curator and staff, a Committee member owes undiluted and positive loyalty to the Governing Body which shares corporate responsibility for the museum, and should never divulge its deliberations and decisions to any outside body or person before they are properly made known to the staff and public. Committee members must accept that decisions are made on majority basis and it is important that members should abide by, rather than undermine these.

1.4   Every Committee member has equal responsibility for the Governing Body's adherence to its own constitution and approved codes, as much as for the Museum's collections, physical 'plant' and property, finances, personnel and all operations. Since no single Chairman or Committee member (as a trustee) can have the authority to act personally, this requires in practice participation in formal delegations to sub-committees, officers or the Director/Curator, and subsequent formal or implicit adoption and endorsement of their actions.

1.5   A Committee member must be satisfied with the regular procedure of preparation and approval of the budgets, including those of any subsidiary commercial activities such as a cafe, museum shop or publications company, and recognise the personal liabilities following on insolvency and 'wrongful or fraudulent trading'. A Committee member should have a regular opportunity to monitor income and expenditure, and staff management procedures.

1.6   A Committee member should be aware of his/her right to raise matters of relevance at any Committee meeting.

1.7   A Committee member should give thought to the need for personal attendance at the Museum's functions and at events run by the institution's friends, associates and other supporters. He/she should also be aware of the museum's working and organisation. In particular a Committee member should recognise that absence from a meeting of the Governing Body may not always absolve from liability for any decision taken thereat in questions of breach of trust or statutory default. Irregular attendance at Committee meetings should be a matter of concern for the Governing Body. A Committee member should always be willing after serving for an appreciable period to volunteer resignation or non-renewal to allow fresh minds to be recruited, without prejudice to possible reappointment later, health and capacity permitting.

The Collections

2.1   A Committee member's prime duty is to be accountable for the long-term safety and professional conservation of the objects in the collections, and/or appropriate additions to them; and to secure their exhibition and interpretation to the public, and availability for legitimate research and study.

2.2   A Committee member should co-operate in promoting the public's awareness, understanding and appreciation of the subjects covered by the Museum's collection, and should collaborate with other institutions as appropriate to provide education, instruction, advice and facilities for research accordingly.

2.3   A Committee member should play a part in ensuring that the Governing Body and Director/Curator follow an agreed collecting policy; this should require full knowledge of the legality of the provenance of acquisitions. There should also be policies on exhibitions, publications, loans borrowings and exchanges, and above all on deaccessioning.

2.4   When considering recommendations on the acquisition of any object a Committee member should take into account the cost implications of its acquisition, in addition to considerations as to whether it will be shown or displayed at specific times and places in the Museum's programme, or retained for a scientific or scholarly purpose in a reserve collection.

2.5   A Committee member should always give priority, before agreeing to disposal of any item which may legally and properly be deaccessioned, to its sale or gift to, or exchange with, another registered museum capable of giving equal service to the interests of the public or students.

2.6   A Committee member should insist on being made aware of any intended major bequests or endowments, the conditions attached to them, and their cost implications, in advance of a decision to acquire them being taken. Governing Body members will be corporately responsible for compliance with any conditions placed on gifts.

2.7   With regard to existing collections, the Governing Body should be made aware of any conditions which may significantly affect the financial, or other responsibilities, of the museum.

The Staff

3.1   The task of Committee member's is to establish (and periodically to review) the policy of the Museum. The task of the Director/Curator is to execute policy and advise on future policy. His/her role is effectively that of the Chief Executive/Managing Director of the organisation. It is the duty of each Committee member and of the Director/Curator not to trespass on each other's territory. The rider is that the Committee member will give the Director/Curator unflinching support so long as the Director/Curator's duties are being carried out effectively and in accordance with the agreed plans and strategy of the museum.

3.2   The Governing Body appoints the Director/Curator (and the Deputy where appropriate), and the latter should have the responsibility for appointing the subordinate staff with whom all must work. In some (particularly large) institutions a Committee member may be called on to represent the Governing Body at the appointment of staff sufficiently senior as to be potential understudies to Director/Curator, or to become involved in an appointment in particular discipline in which a Committee member has special knowledge.

3.3   Following staff representation to the Director the Governing Body should be prepared to hold a final hearing to receive any employee grievances.

3.4   A Committee member is entitled to expect the attendance of the Director/Curator at all Governing Body meetings, unless there are items on the agenda to be kept confidential from all staff (although it would be normal for the Director/Curator to be made aware of the general subject matter through the agenda headings). Committee members are entitled to receive reports and recommendations from the Director/Curator at ordinary meetings concerning the programmes and finances of the museum and the Director/Curator's own current activities.

3.5   In certain circumstances it may be prudent for a Committee member to ensure that independent advice on the desirability of personal insurance against the consequences of accepting inaccurate or imprudent advice from the Museum's officers or staff is taken.

Appendix D *Guidelines for a registration scheme for museums in the United Kingdom*

Introduction – The Advantages and Key Requirements of Registration

1. The experience of museum* development in this century has led to the evolution of a broadly accepted philosophy of how a museum and its functions may be defined. This philosophy centres around the responsibilities a museum owes to its collections and to its public. Although museums in the UK are run by a wide variety of bodies – national and local authorities, universities, charitable societies and private individuals – they hold these responsibilities in common.

2. The Museums Association's *Code of Practice for Museum Authorities* (1977) and *Code of Practice for Curators* (1983) represented the first attempts to define these ideas formally in writing. The Museums & Galleries Commission (MGC) now hopes to take this process a stage further by offering registration to all museums which conform to the guidelines set out in this document. They have been drawn up after wide consultation over a two year period (see 6 below) and represent common standards and aims which may apply to the very largest and to the very smallest museum. We emphasize that they are *guidelines*, and that they will be interpreted in the light of what is reasonable and appropriate in the case of each individual museum. We trust that they will prove to be of positive assistance to small museums and to new museum projects in providing information about the factors to be considered in museum development. At the same time it should be recognised that the guidelines are concerned with minimum standards; it is hoped that most museums will eventually go on to develop their operations far beyond this baseline.

3. Provisional registration will be available to museums which are striving to reach the required standard, and provisionally registered museums will continue to be eligible for grant-aid and subsidised services. The cost implications for most museums will be minimal and there will be no administrative charge associated with registration applications.

4. The advantages of registration can be summarised as follows:

a. eligibility for MGC and Area Museum Council (AMC) grant-aid and subsidised services (see also 39 below);

b. the fostering of confidence among other funding agencies (eg Tourist Boards, charitable foundations and local authorities), that a registered museum is, in principle, worthy of support;

* Throughout this document the term *museum* is used to subsume *gallery*.

c. the fostering of confidence among potential providers of material for a museum's collection that a registered museum is, in principle, a suitable repository;

d. the opportunity for a museum to publicise itself as an organisation which provides a basic range of services for the benefit of its visitors and other users.

5. The key requirements of registration are:

a. accordance with the Museums Association definition of a museum or, if appropriate, the MGC definition of a 'national' museum (see 7–10 below);

b. an acceptable constitution and financial basis, and compliance with all legal and planning requirements (see 12–16 below);

c. publication of an acceptable statement of collection management policy (see 17–21 below);

d. provision of a range of public services/facilities appropriate to the nature, scale and location of the museum (see 22–24 below);

e. access to professional curatorial advice (see 25 & 26 below).

6. The registration scheme as described here has been developed after discussions with the Museums Association, the Association of Independent Museums and the AMC. It was tested on a pilot basis in the North of England during 1986 and further refined after a national consultation exercise. The MGC decision to implement the scheme on a national basis has been widely supported by Government and interested government agencies, the local authority associations, grant-giving bodies and museum bodies.

Definition of a Museum

7. The definition adopted at the Museums Association AGM 1984 was: 'A museum is an institution which collects, documents, preserves, exhibits and interprets material evidence and associated information for the public benefit'. The following guidelines will apply when interpreting this definition for the purposes of the registration scheme.

a. INSTITUTION implies an establishment which has a formal governing instrument and a long-term purpose. Museums and collections privately owned by individuals are not eligible for registration (see also 12–15 & 17–19 below).

b. COLLECTS embraces all means of acquisition. It should also imply the museum's possession of, or intention to acquire, substantial permanent collections in relation to its stated objectives (see also 17–19 below).

c. DOCUMENTS emphasises the obligation to maintain records (see also 20 below).

d. PRESERVES includes all aspects of conservation and security (see also 21 below).

e. EXHIBITS confirms the expectation of visitors that they will be able to see at least a representative selection of objects in the collections. It should also imply that the museum opens to a public at appropriate times and periods (see also 22–24).

f. INTERPRETS covers such diverse fields as display, education, research and publication (see also 22–24 below).

g. MATERIAL indicates something that is tangible, while EVIDENCE indicates its authenticity as the 'real thing'.

h. ASSOCIATED INFORMATION represents the knowledge which prevents a museum object being merely a curio and also includes all records relating to its past history, acquisition and subsequent usage.

i. FOR THE PUBLIC BENEFIT is deliberately open-ended and is intended to reflect the current thinking, both within the museum profession and outside it, that museums are the servants of society. It also implies that a museum should not be a profit-distributing institution, ie it should not distribute profits to shareholders (see also 12 below).

Definition of a 'National' Museum

8. To be eligible for registration, a museum wishing to use the word 'national' or equivalent in its title (see below for list of terms) should conform with the following points:

a. It should conform with the registration scheme.

b. The policy and practice of the museum should be to collect a range of objects of national importance and associated archival material in its particular fields.

c. It should ALREADY have a substantial collection in relation to its stated objectives and the museum display policy should reflect the full range of its collections.

d. It should provide professional and authoritative expertise and advice in all its fields to the public and other museums.

e. It should provide study and research facilities for the public.

Museums constituted as charitable companies should note that the Companies Act 1985 provides statutory constraints to the use of terms such as 'national' in company names.

9. The following names should be regarded as equivalent to 'national' and therefore subject to the above-mentioned criteria: International; World; Nation; Europe; European; United Kingdom; Great Britain; Britain; British; England; English; Scotland; Scottish; Wales; Welsh; Ulster; Northern Ireland; Northern Irish.

10. EXCEPTIONS: there are institutions which have the term 'National', 'British', etc, incorporated into their titles by statute or Royal Charter. If one of these establishes a museum, it may of right use its official title in the name of its museum, eg British Telecom Museum.

Institutions ineligible for Independent Registration but eligible for Registration as part of a broadly-based Museum Service

11. The following categories of institution will not be deemed eligible for registration unless they form part of a broadly-based museum service which conforms with the registration guidelines:

a. science centres and planetaria;

b. natural, archaeological, historical, and industrial monuments and sites, not having associated museum collections;

c. institutions displaying live specimens, eg zoos and aquaria;

d. educational loan services;

e. record offices;

f. venues for temporary exhibitions;

g. biological and environmental record centres.

Constitutions

12. The following constitutions will be deemed acceptable:

a. those based on Local Government Acts and forming the subject of a Local Authority Resolution;

b. those based on any other Act of Parliament;

c. those based on the formal decision of any public body;

d. those based on the formal decision of a university senate or council;

e. those based on an ACCEPTABLE memorandum and articles of a charitable company;

f. those based on an ACCEPTABLE deed of trust of a charitable trust;

g. any other constitution which is acceptable to the MGC and which meets the criteria set out in this document, including the non-distribution of any profits. Commercial and company museums will be eligible provided that any profits made by the museum are retained within the museum.

13. With reference to categories e. and f., examples of acceptable formats are:

a. conformance with the specimen drafts published in the Association of Independent Museums Guideline No. 3, 'Charitable Status for Museums' (both versions: i. Scotland ii. Rest of UK);

b. conformance with the specimen trust deed published by the Army Museums Ogilby Trust.

14. It is recognised that these specimen trust deeds (13. a. & b.) do not adequately provide for the safeguarding of museum collections. To counter this deficiency it is necessary for a museum's governing body formally to adopt the clauses in the registration guidelines which refer to the disposal of collections (see 18. f.–j. below).

Finances

15. A museum should be able to demonstrate that it has a sound financial basis and a copy of the current annual budget should be provided. Independent museums should also submit financial accounts for the two most recent financial years; these should include income and expenditure accounts and a balance sheet, and distinguish between annual operating costs/income, and details of commitments undertaken and financial resources available to meet development costs. Accounts must either be audited or, in the case of private trusts not legally required to provide audited accounts, certified appropriately. A museum should be sufficiently well supported and financially viable irrespective of any valuation placed on the items in its collection. In no circumstances should those items be mortgaged or in any way held as security for any loan. Information concerning the status of the museum building or site housing the collections should also be provided (eg leasehold, freehold).

Legal, Safety and Planning Requirements

16. Museum governing bodies are required to undertake that they have ensured and will continue to ensure that all relevant legal, safety and planning requirements are complied with.

Collection Management Policy

17. The policy statement should provide the following information:

a. details of the museum's acquisition and disposal policy;

b. the nature of the museum's existing collection;

c. details concerning the documentation of the collection;

d. access to professional conservation advice.

ACQUISITION & DISPOSAL POLICY

18. A museum's acquisition and disposal policy must be formally approved by the governing body. SUB-PARAGRAPHS b. to j. INCLUSIVE (below), OR EQUIVALENT WORDING, SHOULD BE INCORPORATED WITHIN THE POLICY. They are based upon a section of the Museums Association *Code of Practice for Museum Authorities*. Evidence of formal approval should be supplied in the form of a committee minute signed by a properly authorised person. This person should be the Chief Executive or proper officer authorised by the governing body (Local Authority Museums); the Chairman, Secretary or other person authorised by the governing body (Independent and National Museums); the Vice-Chancellor, Registrar or other person authorised by the governing body (University Museums).

a. Reference should be made to the nature of the collections and the criteria used to define their scope. The criteria should normally include the following: the subjects or themes of the collection; the period of time and/or geographical area from which the collection is derived; the limitations on collecting imposed by such factors as inadequate staffing, storage and conservation. Due account should be taken of the collecting policies of other museums in order to avoid unnecessary duplication and waste of resources.

b. The acquisition policy should be published and reviewed from time to time, at least once every five years. Acquisitions outside the current stated policy should only be made in very exceptional circumstances, and then only after proper consideration by the governing body of the museum itself, having regard to the interests of other museums. The AMC should be notified of any changes to the acquisitions policy.

c. A museum should not acquire, whether by purchase, gift, bequest or exchange, any work of art or object unless the governing body or responsible officer is satisfied that the museum can acquire a valid title to the specimen in question, and that in particular it has not been acquired in, or exported from, its country of origin (or any intermediate country in which it may have been legally owned) in violation of that country's laws. (For the purpose of this paragraph 'country of origin' includes the United Kingdom).

d. So far as biological and geological material is concerned, a museum should not acquire by any direct or indirect means any specimen that has been collected, sold or otherwise transferred in contravention of any national or international wildlife protection or natural history conservation law or treaty of the United Kingdom or any other country, except with the express consent of an appropriate outside authority (eg a British court in the case of a specimen seized from a third party under the Protection of Birds Acts).

e. So far as British or foreign archaeological antiquities (including excavated ceramics) are concerned, in addition to the safeguards under sub-paragraph c. above, the museum should not acquire by purchase objects in any case where the governing body or responsible officer has reasonable cause to believe that the circumstances of their recovery involved the recent unscientific or intentional destruction or damage of ancient monuments or other known archaeological sites, or involved a failure to disclose the finds to the owner or occupier of the land, or to the proper authorities in the case of a possible Treasure Trove (in England and Wales) or Bona Vacantia (Scotland).

f. By definition (see 7 above), a museum should have a long-term purpose and possess (or intend to acquire) substantial permanent collections in relation to its stated objectives. Each museum authority must accept the principle that there is a strong presumption against the disposal of any items in the museum's collection except as set out below.

g. In those cases where a museum is free to dispose of an item (eg by virtue of an Act of Parliament or of permission from the High Court or the Charity Commissioners), it should be agreed that any decision to sell or dispose of material from the collections should be taken only after due consideration by the museum's governing body, and such material should be offered first, by loan, exchange, gift or sale to registered museums before sale to other interested individuals or organisations is considered.

h. In cases in which an arrangement for the exchange, gift or private treaty sale of material is not being made with an individual museum, the museum community at large must be advised of the intention to dispose of material. This should normally be through an announcement in the Museums Association's *Museums Journal*. The announcement should indicate the number of specimens involved, the prime objects concerned and the basis on which the material would be transferred to another institution. A period of at least two months must be allowed for an interest in acquiring the material to be expressed.

i. A decision to dispose of a specimen or work of art, whether by exchange, sale, gift or destruction (in the case of an item too badly damaged or deteriorated to be of any use for the purposes of the collections), should be the responsibility of the governing body of the museum acting on the advice of professional curatorial staff, and not of the curator of the collection concerned acting alone. Full records should be kept of all such decisions and the specimens involved and proper arrangements made for the preservation and/or transfer, as appropriate, of the documentation relating to the object concerned, including photographic records where practicable.

j. Any monies received by a governing body from the disposal of specimens or works of art should be applied for the benefit of the museum collections. This should normally mean the purchase of exhibits for the collections but in exceptional cases improvements relating to the care of collections may be justifiable. Advice on these cases may be sought from the MGC.

NATURE OF THE MUSEUM'S EXISTING COLLECTION

19. Details should be provided of the EXISTING collection, indicating the proportion of items on loan to the museum.

DOCUMENTATION OF THE COLLECTION

20. Details of the museum's documentation system should be provided. The minimum requirement is as follows:

a. the maintenance of entry records of all items deposited in the museum, eg as enquiries, loans or potential acquisitions;

b. the maintenance of a register with records about all accessions and long-term loans, each including an accession or inventory number and sufficient information for collections management purposes;

c. the marking or labelling of each accession and (where appropriate) each individual object with a unique accession or inventory number;

d. the maintenance of one or more indexes or equivalent information retrieval facilities, including (where appropriate) subject, donor and location lists;

e. if documentation of the collection has not been completed as set out above, a statement of the museum's policy to eliminate this backlog within a stated timescale should be provided.

CONSERVATION OF THE COLLECTIONS

21. Minimum standards are not proposed AT THIS STAGE, but all reasonable steps should be taken to preserve the collections. Access to professional conservation advice is essential and details of the person(s)/ organisation(s) normally consulted should be provided (see also 25 and 26 below relating to curatorial advice).

Public Services

22. The museum should provide a range of public services appropriate to its nature and scale relating to the interpretation of its collections; eg temporary exhibitions, educational activities and publications. Details should be provided.

23. In addition, the museum should provide or have available in the immediate vicinity a reasonable range of visitor facilities appropriate to the scale, location and nature of the museum; eg parking, toilet, catering and disabled access facilities. Details should be provided.

24. A museum should normally be open to the general public. If the museum's public is restricted, this must be defined, but will not automatically rule out acceptance for registration. Details should be provided of opening hours or other arrangements for access, and the means by which this information is advertised.

Staffing and access to Professional Curatorial Advice

25. The governing body has a special obligation to ensure that the museum has staff sufficient in both number and kind to ensure that the museum is able to meet its responsibilities. Proper arrangements should be made for the museum to meet its obligations in relation to the care of the collections, public access and services, research and security. The size of the staff, and its nature (whether paid or unpaid, permanent or temporary), will depend on the size of the museum, its collections and its responsibilities.

26. A formal statement will be required which conforms with the following guidelines:

a. A museum's governing body should normally have the services of a professionally trained and/or experienced curator; ie someone holding a degree and/or the Diploma of the Museums Association or equivalent qualifications and/or substantial relevant experience. Full details should be submitted. (Interpretation of 'equivalent qualifications and/or substantial relevant experience' will be determined by the MGC in the light of case studies derived from the pilot registration scheme 1985–86). There should be an efficient line of communication between the curator and the appropriate committee of the museum's governing body. We would normally expect that the senior museum professional is allowed direct access to the appropriate committee at least when estimates are presented and museum policy discussed. Details of these arrangements should be submitted.

b. In the case of a SMALL museum which does not have the services of a professionally trained and/or experienced curator (as described above), the museum's governing body should make arrangements to receive curatorial advice from such a person on a regular basis. Normally, this would be done by appointing such a person to be a full member of the governing body. Alternatively, a curatorial adviser may be appointed (the AMC will be able to advise on potential curatorial advisers). Evidence of the formal appointment of a curatorial adviser by a museum's governing body should be provided in the form of a committee minute signed by a properly authorised person (see 18 above). All minutes and papers for meetings of the governing body should be sent to the curatorial adviser who should also be offered the opportunity to attend such meetings. The curatorial adviser (or the Board member who fulfils this role) will be expected to endorse the registration application and make an annual report to the AMC concerning the operation of the museum and its continued con-formance with the registration criteria. Normally, only the smallest museums should find it necessary to take advantage of these arrange-ments and interpretation of 'small' will be determined by the MGC in the light of case studies derived from the pilot registration scheme.

Registration and Appeals Procedure

27. Registration application forms should be completed and returned to the Area Museum Council within 6 months from the start of the scheme as advised by the MGC (see also 35 below).

28. Within a further 6 month period the Director of the AMC will send all applications to the MGC.

29. Applicants will be considered by a registration committee drawn from a pool of nominated members. Any meeting of the committee will comprise:

a. Two representatives of the MGC, drawn from a group which will comprise two Commissioners (one of whom will be the Committee's official Chairman), the Director, and the Deputy Director; any one of these four shall be entitled to take the chair at a meeting;

b. A museum professional appointed after consultation with the President of the Museums Association;

c. A museum professional appointed after consultation with the Chairman of the Association of Independent Museums;

d. A representative of the relevant AMC.

30. The registration committee will be able to co-opt expert advisers on an *ad hoc* basis when specialist advice on particular categories of museum is required.

31. the MGC will notify museums of their registration or the reasons for their rejection. Provisional registration may be offered to museums which are striving to reach registration standard, subject to annual review, eg museums at an early stage of development.

32. Museums which fail to qualify for registration will be notified of their right to appeal. Any appeals must be received by the MGC within 6 months of the date of the rejection letter. The appeals committee will comprise two Commissioners and a museum professional nominated by the Museums Association; none of them previously involved in the decision to reject the applicant.

33. Whilst registration confers eligibility to receive funds from the MGC and the AMC, the acceptance of a museum under the registration scheme does not commit the MGC or any AMC to provide funding or to accept any responsibility for the management of the museum concerned.

34. Registered museums will be allocated a unique registration number which can be quoted on all published material. A certificate will also be provided.

35. Late applicants will not be excluded from the registration scheme but the processing of their application forms may be delayed. New museums established after the initial registration period may apply to be registered at any time.

Access to the Register and Maintenance

36. The register of museums will be maintained at the MGC. Copies will be made available to AMCs, to other agencies concerned with the funding of museums, and to the Museums Association and the Association of Independent Museums. All copies of the register will be available for inspection by enquirers with a BONA FIDE interest.

37. The MGC reserves the right to remove a museum from the register at any time if it can be shown that it no longer conforms with the criteria in the guidelines. Such decisions will be made after an appropriate period of written notice and subject to the normal appeals procedure. A museum may also request that it be removed from the register if it so desires.

38. Registered museums will be expected to make an annual statistical return to their AMC confirming/amending previously submitted particulars. Museums will be expected to renew their applications for registration at five yearly intervals, commencing from the initial registration date.

Other Organisations eligible for MGC and AMC Funding

39. The following categories of organisation providing specialist services of repute for museums will be deemed eligible for financial support from the MGC and AMCs notwithstanding their ineligibility for registration:

a. countywide, regional, and nationwide museum advisory services;

b. reputable conservation services;

c. reputable museum-related training centres.

29 February 1988

Appendix E *Museums Association Code of Practice for Museum Authorities*

1. Introduction

1.1 The Museums Association was founded in 1889 as an organisation comprising and representing museums and art galleries and the staff who work in them, both in the British Isles and overseas. Thus it has both Institutional and Personal Members.

Membership is open also to persons connected with, or interested in, museums, who are not professionally engaged in museum work, and to certain classes of institutions which do not themselves own museums, but which are in some way connected with the Museums Service.

1.2 The principal aims of the Association are to promote the establishment and better administration of museums and galleries and to improve the qualifications and status of members of museum staffs. It furthers these aims by the arrangement of conferences and meetings, by the collection and reporting of information about museums in its publications, including 'Museums Journal' (published monthly), 'Museums Yearbook' (annual), and other literature, and by the organisation of professional and technical training which leads to recognised qualifications for museum staff.

1.3 It represents the interests of museums and the museum profession with governmental and other outside bodies, whether public or private, national or foreign. It maintains links with UNESCO and the International Council of Museums and collaborates with the Museums and Galleries Commission, the Arts Council, the Council for British Archaeology, the Local Authority Associations, the Countryside Commission and similar organisations in related fields of study. The Association works closely with the Area Museum Councils which provide, with the aid of central government grant-in-aid, technical and advisory services to museums in their areas, with the regional Museums Federations and with the specialist professional groups in affiliation.

1.4 Throughout its existence the Association has offered guidance to all charged with the specific function of trusteeship of museums and art galleries, an essential part of the heritage, on practical, ethical and professional matters relating to the management of museums and the care and development of their collections. Over the past ten years in particular, guidance has been issued on a wide range of important topics, and in the light of the developing policy of the Association this Code of Practice for Museum Authorities adopted by the Annual General Meeting of the Association of 16 July 1977 and amended by the Annual General Meeting on 24 July 1987, is now commended to boards of trustees, local authorities, museum committees, senior staff and others involved in the management of museums and art galleries.

2. Definition of a museum

'A museum is an institution which collects, documents, preserves, exhibits and interprets material evidence and associated information for the public benefit.'

EXPLANATION

Every effort has been made to include all the basic functions of a museum in as few words as possible. 'Institution' implies a formalised establishment which has a long-term purpose. 'Collects' embraces all means of acquisition. 'Documents' emphasises the need to maintain records. 'Preserves' includes all aspects of conservation and security. 'Exhibits' confirms the expectation of visitors that they will be able to see at least a representative selection of the objects in the collections. 'Interprets' is taken to cover such diverse fields as display, education, research and publication. 'Material' indicates something that is tangible, while 'Evidence' guarantees its authenticity as the 'real thing'. 'Associated information' represents the knowledge which prevents a museum object being merely a curio, and also includes all records relating to its past history, acquisition and subsequent usage. 'For the public benefit' is deliberately open ended and is intended to reflect the current thinking, both within our profession and outside it, that museums are the servants of society.

3. Basic principles for museum governance

3.1   The governing body or other controlling authority of a museum has an ethical duty to maintain, and if possible enhance, all aspects of the museum, its collections and its services. Above all, it is the responsibility of each governing body to ensure that all of the collections in their care are adequately housed, conserved and documented. The minimum standards in terms of finance, premises, staffing and services will vary according to the size and responsibility of each museum. Guidance on these can be obtained from the Museums and Galleries Commission, the Area Museum Councils, the Museums Association and various specialist professional bodies and groups.

3.2   Each museum should have a written constitution or other document setting out clearly its legal status and permanent, non-profit nature, drawn up in accordance with appropriate national laws in relation to museums, the cultural heritage and non-profit institutions. The governing body or other controlling authority of a museum should prepare and publicise a clear statement of the aims, objectives and policies of the museum and of the role and composition of the governing body itself.

3.3   The governing body holds the ultimate financial responsibility for the museum and for the protecting and nurturing of its various assets: the collections and related documentation, the premises, facilities and equipment, the financial assets and the staff. It is obliged to develop and define the purposes and related policies of the institution, and ensure that all of the museum's assets are properly and effectively used for museum purposes. Sufficient funds must be available on a regular basis, either from public or private sources, to enable the governing body to carry out and develop the work of the museum. Proper accounting procedures must be adopted and maintained in accordance with the relevant national laws and professional accountancy standards.

3.4 The governing body has specially strong obligations to provide accommodation giving a suitable environment for the physical security and preservation of the collections. Premises must be adequate for the museum to fulfil within its stated policy its basic functions of collection, research, storage, conservation, education and display, including staff accommodation, and should comply with all appropriate national legislation in relation to public and staff safety. Proper standards of protection should be provided against such hazards as theft, fire, flood, vandalism and deterioration, throughout the year, day and night. The special needs of disabled people should be provided for, as far as practicable, in planning and managing both buildings and facilities.

3.5 The governing body has a special obligation to ensure that the museum has staff sufficient in both number and kind to ensure that the museum is able to meet its responsibilities. The size of the staff, and its nature (whether paid or unpaid, permanent or temporary), will depend on the size of the museum, its collections and its responsibilities.However, proper arrangements should be made for the museum to meet its obligations in relation to the care of the collections, public access and services, research and security. The governing body has particularly important obligations in relation to the appointment of the director of the museum, and whenever the possibility of terminating the employment of the director arises, to ensure that any such action is taken only in accordance with appropriate procedures under the legal or other constitutional arrangements and policies of the museum, and that any such staff changes are made in a professional and ethical manner, and in accordance with what is judged to be the best interests of the museum, rather than any personal or external factor or prejudice. It should also ensure that the same principles are applied in relation to any appointment, promotion, dismissal or demotion of the personnel of the museum by the director or any other senior member of staff with staffing responsibilities.

The governing body should recognise the diverse nature of the museum profession and the wide range of specialisations that it now encompasses, including conservator/restorers, scientists, museum education service personnel, registrars and computer specialists, security service managers, etc. It should ensure that the museum both makes appropriate use of such specialists where required and that such specialised personnel are properly recognised as full members of the professional staff in all respects. Members of the museum profession require appropriate academic, technical and professional training in order to fulfil their important role in relation to the operation of the museum and the care for the heritage, and the governing body should recognise the need for, and value of, a properly qualified and trained staff, and offer adequate opportunities for further training and re-training in order to maintain an adequate and effective workforce.

The director or other chief professional officer of a museum should be directly responsible to, and have direct access to, the governing body in which trusteeship of the collections is vested.

3.6   By definition a museum is an institution in the service of society and of its development, and is generally open to the public (even though this may be a restricted public in the case of certain very specialised museums, such as certain academic or medical museums, for example).

The museum should take every opportunity to develop its role as an educational resource used by all sections of the population or specialised group that the museum is intended to serve. Where appropriate in relation to the museum's programme and responsibilities specialist staff with training and skills in museum education are likely to be required for this purpose. The museum has an important duty to attract new and wider audiences within all levels of the community, locality or group that the museum aims to serve, and should offer both the general community and specific individuals and groups within it opportunities to be actively involved in the museum and to support its aims and policies.

3.7   The general public (or specialised group served, in the case of museums with a limited public role) should have access to the displays during reasonable hours and for regular periods. The museum should also offer the public reasonable access to members of staff by appointment or other arrangements and full access to information about the collections, subject to any necessary restrictions for reasons of confidentiality or security.

3.8   Subject to the primary duty of the museum to preserve unimpaired for the future the significant material that comprises the museum collections, it is the responsibility of the museum to use the collections for the creation and dissemination of new knowledge, through research, educational work, permanent displays, temporary exhibitions and other special activities. These should be in accordance with the stated policy and educational purpose of the museum, and should not compromise either the quality or the proper care of the collections. The museum should seek to ensure that information in display and exhibitions is honest and objective and does not perpetuate myths of stereotypes.

3.9   Where it is the policy of the museum to seek and accept financial or other support from commercial or industrial organisations, or from other outside sources, great care is needed to define clearly the agreed relationship between the museum and the sponsor. Commercial support and sponsorship may involve ethical problems and the museum must ensure that the standards and objectives of the museum are not compromised by such a relationship.

3.10 Museum shops and any other commercial activities of the museum, and any publicity relating to these, should be in accordance with a clear policy, should be relevant to the collections and the basic educational purpose of the museum, and must not compromise the quality of those collections. In the case of the manufacture and sale of replicas, reproductions or other commercial items adapted from an object in a museum's collection, all aspects of the commercial venture must be carried out in a manner that will not discredit either the integrity of the museum or the intrinsic value of the original object. Great care must be taken to identify permanently such objects for what they are, and to ensure accuracy and high quality in their manufacture. All items offered for sale should represent good value for money and should comply with all relevant national legislation.

3.11 It is an important responsibility of each governing body to ensure that the museum complies fully with all legal obligations, whether in relation to national, regional or local law, international law or treaty obligations, and to any legally binding trusts or conditions relating to any aspect of the museum collections or facilities.

4. Acquisitions to museum and art gallery collections

4.1 The Museums Association has been actively co-operating for many years with UNESCO and the International Council of Museums and fully supports international efforts to control and eliminate international trafficking in stolen and illegally exported works of art, antiquities and other museum objects.

4.2 The United Kingdom already has treaty obligations under the 'European Convention on the Protection of the Archaeological Heritage' adopted in March 1973 (Cmnd. 5224) but in addition the Association supports the principle of the much wider UNESCO 'Convention of the Means of Prohibiting and Preventing the Illicit Import, Export and Transfer of Ownership of Cultural Property' 1970, and will continue to press the United Kingdom Government to ratify and enact the 'Convention'.

4.3 The Association considers it essential that notwithstanding the fact that the UNESCO 'Convention' has not yet been ratified by the United Kingdom each museum should comply with the terms and ethical principles of the 'Convention' so far as these are applicable to an individual museum authority.

4.4 Each museum authority should adopt and publish a written statement of its acquisitions policy. This policy should be reviewed from time to time, at least once every five years. Acquisitions outside the current stated policy should only be made in very exceptional circumstances, and then only after proper consideration by the governing body of the museum itself, having regard to the interest of other museums.

4.5　A museum should not acquire, whether by purchase, gift, bequest or exchange, any work of art or object unless the governing body or responsible officer as appropriate is satisfied that the museum can acquire a valid title to the specimen in question and that in particular it has not been acquired in, or exported from, its country of origin (and/or any intermediate country in which it may have been legally owned) in violation of that country's laws. (For the purpose of this paragraph 'country of origin' shall include the United Kingdom.)

4.6　So far as biological and geological material is concerned a museum should not acquire by any direct or indirect means any specimen that has been collected, sold or otherwise transferred in contravention of any national or international wildlife protection or natural history conservation law or treaty of the United Kingdom or any other country except with the express consent of an appropriate outside authority (eg a British court in the case of a specimen seized from a third party under the Protection of Birds Acts).

4.7　So far as British or foreign archaeological antiquities (including excavated ceramics) are concerned, in addition to the safeguards under para. 4.5 above, the museum should not acquire by purchase objects in any case where the governing body or responsible officer has reasonable cause to believe that the circumstances of their recovery involved the recent unscientific or intentional destruction or damage of ancient monuments or other known archaeological sites, or involved a failure to disclose the finds to the owner or occupier of the land, or to the proper authorities in the case of possible Treasure Trove (in England and Wales) or Bona Vacantia (Scotland).

4.8　Special attention is drawn to Articles 6(2) (a) and 6(2)(b) of the European Convention on the Protection of the Archaeological Heritage: '2. Each Contracting Party undertakes specifically:
(a) as regards museums and other similar institutions whose acquisition policy is under State control, to take the necessary measures to avoid their acquiring archaeological objects suspected, for a specific reason, of having originated from clandestine excavations or of coming unlawfully from official excavations;
(b) as regards museums and other similar institutions, situated in the territory of a Contracting Party but enjoying freedom from state control in their acquisition policy:
(i) to transmit the text of this Convention, and (ii) to spare no effort to obtain the support of the said museums and institutions for the principles set out in the preceding paragraph.'

4.9　If appropriate and feasible the same tests as are outlined in the above four paragraphs should be applied in determining whether to accept loans for exhibition or other purposes.

4.10　Each museum authority should recognise the need for co-operation and consultation between all museums and galleries, both national and provincial, with similar or overlapping interests and collecting policies and should seek to consult with such other institutions both on specific acquisitions where a conflict of interests is thought possible and, more generally, on defining areas of specialisation.

4.11   If a museum should in future come into the possession of an object that can be demonstrated to have been exported or otherwise transferred in violation of the principles of the UNESCO 'Convention' and the country of origin seeks its return and demonstrates that it is part of the country's cultural heritage, the museum should, if legally free to do so, take responsible steps to co-operate in the return of the object to the country of origin.

4.12   Special attention is drawn to the following statement issued in May 1972:
The Standing Commission on Museums and Galleries, in consultation with the British Academy, the British Museum and the Museums Association (representing the other relevant museums in the United Kingdom), having considered the UNESCO 'Convention on the Means of Prohibiting and Preventing the Illicit Import, Export and Transfer of Ownership of Cultural Property, adopted in Paris in November 1970, and the aims underlying it, declare that:
  (i) they attach the highest importance to preventing the destruction of the records of man's past and the despoliation of archaeological and other historical sites;
  (ii) they recognise the importance, in the scientific and scholarly study and interchange of archaeological and other cultural material, of mutual confidence and assistance between countries concerned and will do everything in their power to promote it;
  (iii) they affirm that it is and will continue to be the practice of museums and galleries in the United Kingdom that they do not and will not knowingly acquire any antiquities or other cultural material which they have reason to believe has been exported in contravention of the current laws of the country of origin.'

4.13   Many museums and galleries have experienced great difficulty from time to time because of special conditions and restrictions on items in their collections (eg that items will be permanently displayed, shown in separate rooms, etc). The Association does not recommend the acceptance of a gift or bequest to which any special conditions apply (except for conditions intended to assure the permanent protection of the item in the collection, such as restrictions on any legal power of disposal that the museum or gallery may have). The use of the term 'permanent loan' has no legal status.

4.14   The collecting policy or regulations of the museum should include provisions to ensure that no person involved in the policy or management of the museum, such as a trustee or other member of a governing body, or a member of the museums staff may compete with the museum for objects or may take advantage of privileged information received because of his or her position, and that should a conflict of interest develop between the needs of the individual and the museum, those of the museum will prevail. Special care is also required in considering any offer of an item either for sale or as a tax-benefit gift, from members of governing bodies, members of staff or the families or close associates of these.

5. Disposal of collections

5.1   The definition of a museum in para. 2 makes it clear that it is a key function of a museum or art gallery to acquire objects and/or works of art and to keep them for posterity. Consequently there must be a strong presumption against the disposal of any items in the collections of a museum.

5.2   A number of the most important national museums and galleries are governed under Acts of Parliament which specifically prohibit the disposal of items in the collections and, even where this is not the case, various severe restrictions are placed on the powers to dispose of items from the museum or gallery.

5.3   So far as local authority and private trust museums and galleries are concerned, attention is drawn to the important advice on the legal position included in the 'Report of the Committee of Enquiry into the Sale of Works of Art by Public Bodies' (HMSO 1964) as follows:

The basic principle upon which the law rests is that when private persons give property for public purposes the Crown undertakes to see that it is devoted to the purposes intended by the donor, and to no others. When a work of art is given to a museum or gallery for general exhibition, the public thereby acquires rights in the object concerned and these rights cannot be set aside. The authorities of the museum or gallery are not the owners of such an object in the ordinary sense of the word: they are merely responsible, under the authority of the Courts, for carrying out the intentions of the donor. They cannot sell the object unless authorised to do so by the Courts or by the Charity Commissioners or the Minister of Education on behalf of the Courts, because they have themselves nothing to sell. If they attempt a sale in breach of trust it is the function of the Attorney General to enforce the trust and protect the rights of the public in the object by taking proceedings in the 'Chancery Division.'

5.4   It should also be stressed that even where general powers of disposal exist a museum or art gallery may not be completely free to dispose of items purchased where financial assistance has been obtained from an outside source (for example central government grant-in-aid, National Art-Collections Fund, Friends of the Museum organisation or a private benefactor) disposal would require the consent of all parties who had contributed to the purchase.

5.5.   In those cases where a museum is free to dispose of an item (eg by virtue of a local Act of Parliament or of permission from the High Court or the Charity Commissioners) any decision to sell or dispose of material from the collections should be taken only after due consideration, and such material should be offered first, by exchange, gift or private treaty sale, to other museums before sale by public auction is considered.

5.6   In cases in which an arrangement for the exchange, gift or private treaty sale of material is not being made with an individual museum, the museum community at large must be advised of the intention to dispose of material through an announcement in *Museums Journal*. The announcement must indicate the number of specimens involved, the prime objects concerned and the basis on which the material would be transferred to another institution. A period of at least two months must be allowed for an interest in acquiring the material to be expressed.

5.7   A decision to dispose of a specimen or work of art, whether by exchange, sale or destruction (in the case of an item too badly damaged or deteriorated to be restorable), should be the responsibility of the governing body of the museum acting on the advice of professional curatorial staff and not of the curator of the collection concerned acting alone. Full records should be kept of all such decisions and the specimens involved and proper arrangements made for the preservation and/or transfer, as appropriate, of the documentation relating to the object concerned, including photographic records where practicable.

5.8   Any monies received by a governing body from the disposal of specimens or works of art should be applied solely for the purchase of additions to the museum or art gallery collections.

6. Museum Organisation

6.1   Over a period of more than fifty years a series of independent reports have consistently supported the view of the Museums Association that the curator or director of a museum or art gallery should be directly responsible and have direct access to the governing body in which trusteeship of the collections is vested.

6.2   The Wright Committee, in its Report to the Minister for the Arts (Provincial Museums and Galleries, HMSO 1973) discussed the Bains 'Report on the Management and structure of the New Local Authorities' and stated:

'12.2   We have seen and heard of a good many cases in which museums, even if they are provided with professionally qualified staff, are administered by librarians. We discuss in Chapter 6 the levels of training and expertise required of a museum curator, and consider that curatorial decisions within museums should be taken by staff who possess such expertise. Despite the valuable links which can be forged between libraries and museums we believe that efficiency is generally better served, if museums are administered separately.

12.3   In any case we are convinced by the argument for a museum director or curator having direct access to the appropriate committee, at least when estimates are presented and museum policy discussed. Even if for administrative purposes the director is a subordinate of some other officer this should always be made possible.'

6.3   The Museums Association considers that precisely the same criteria should apply in other circumstances (eg where the museum or gallery is part of a local authority recreation department or, indeed, a part only of the activities of a more general charitable trust). The Association is of the firm opinion that the only means of ensuring efficient operation and development of the service is for the curator/director to be a chief officer with direct access to the governing body and, in any case, regardless of the status of the most senior professional, the following minimum standards should apply:

(a) a competently trained and qualified Curator should be responsible for the services and staff of the museum and/or art gallery;

(b) the Curator should be responsible for compiling reports and submitting them in person to the governing body or committee;

(c) the Curator should be responsible for preparing and controlling annual estimates, and participating in their presentation to the governing body or committee;

(d) the Curator should be concerned with the preparation of capital development schemes and the submission of agreed capital estimates to the governing body;

(e) a properly qualified Curator should be paid at a salary commensurate with her/his specialised qualifications, professional experience and the responsibilities she/he has for the collections which are normally of high monetary, artistic or scientific value.

7. Responsibility to the Curator

The employing body should pursue a policy that allows the curator to act in accordance with the *Code of Conduct for Museum Curators*. The employing body should never require the curator to act in a way that would reasonably be judged to conflict with the provisions of her/his professional Code.

Appendix F *Museums Association Policy on Admission Charges*

Museums and galleries form part of Britain's internationally-renowned cultural heritage. The tradition of free access to the collections of our publicly-funded museums and galleries is as important and integral a component of the Nation's academic, educational and cultural life as are free library and education services.

The Museums Association asserts that both central and local Government have an overriding responsibility to maintain the tradition of free access to their museums and galleries. They should not therefore apply pressure on these institutions to introduce admission charges in order to meet their most basic running costs.

The decision whether or not to charge for admission must be one for each individual museum to make, taking into account its location, the appeal of its collections, the likely impact on its public and its financial situation. In circumstances in which an admission charge to publicly-funded museums is levied, it is the policy of Museums Association that the following principles should be applied:

1. All revenue raised should be used for the direct benefit of the museum in addition to its revenue income and the accounts of the museum whether in the public or independent sector should clearly demonstrate that this has been done.

2. To facilitate the broadest possible access to collections:

(a) Free admission should be provided for the equivalent of at least one day a week.

(b) Reduced rates should be available for children, senior citizens, disabled people, students and the unemployed at all times. The Museums Association recognizes the growth of museums in the independent sector, which have often been established on the basis of admission charges forming a major part of their income.

In view of the excellent work carried out by many of these institutions and recognizing their role both as employers and as part of the tourist industry, the Museums Association does not propose that they should be discouraged from charging for admission.

Appendix G *List of published sources*

The Drew Report: *Framework for a System for Museums*. Museums & Galleries Commission, London: HMSO, 1978

The Wright Report: *Provincial Museums and Galleries*. Department of Education and Science, London: HMSO, 1973

Museums in Scotland. Museums & Galleries Commission, London: HMSO, 1986

Review of Area Museum Councils and Services. Museums & Galleries Commission, London: HMSO, 1984

Countywide Consultative Committees for Museums. Museums & Galleries Commission, London: HMSO, 1982

New Visions for Independent Museums in the UK. Victor T.C. Middleton, Association of Independent Museums, 1990

The Museums of the Armed Services. Museums & Galleries Commission, London: HMSO, 1990

The Forward Planning Handbook. Routledge, 1991

Managing Services Effectively – Performance Review. Audit Commission, 1989

Management of Performance, a Manager's Guide. The Society of Chief Personnel Officers, 1989

The Road to Wigan Pier? Managing Local Authority Museums and Art Galleries. Audit Commission, London; HMSO, 1991

Volunteers in Museums and Heritage Organisations. London: HMSO, 1991

Museum Professional Training and Career Structure. Museums & Galleries Commission, London: HMSO, 1987

The Conservation of Industrial Collections. J.D. Storer London: Conservation Unit of Museums and Galleries Commission and The Science Museum, 1989

A Conservation Survey of Museum Collections in Scotland. Brian Ramer, Scottish Museum Council, 1989

Museums and Galleries Commission Annual Report 1989–90. Museums & Galleries Commission, London: 1990

Principles for good practice in arts sponsorship. London: Association for Business Sponsorship of the Arts, 1990

Museums UK. London: The Museums Association, 1987

Tax Effective Giving to the Arts & Museums: A Guide to Fundraisers. Arts Council and Museums & Galleries Commission, 1990

The National Curriculum: A Guide for Staff of Museums, Galleries, Historic Houses and Sites. National Curriculum Council, 1990

Museums and the Curriculum. London: Area Museums Service for South Eastern England, 1988

Arts and Schools. London: Office of Arts and Libraries/Department of Education and Science/HMSO, 1990

Initiatives in Museum Education. ed. Eilean Hooper-Greenhill, Department of Museum Studies, University of Leicester, 1989

A Survey of the Use Schools Make of Museums Across the Curriculum. London: DES, 1989 HMI Report 340/89

A Survey of the Use of Museums in Primary Phase Courses in Initial Teacher Training. London: DES, 1990

A Survey of the Use Schools Make of Museums for Learning about Ethnic and Cultural Diversity. London: DES, 1988 HMI Report 163/89

Black Contribution to History. The Geffrye Museum, 1988

A Survey of the Use Some Pupils and Students with Special Education Needs Make of Museums and Historic Buildings. London: DES, 1987, HMI Report 4/88

Security for Museums. Nell Hoare, Committee of Area Museum Councils in association with the Museums Association, 1990

The Economic Importance of the Arts in Britain. John Myerscough, London: Policy Studies Institute, 1988

Think Rural: Act Now. London: Arts Council of Great Britain 1989

Appendix H *Bodies and individuals who submitted written or oral evidence*

Area Museums Council for the South West

Area Museums Service for South Eastern England

Arts Council of Great Britain

Association of Suffolk Museums

Association of District Councils

Association of London Authorities

Association of Metropolitan Authorities

Frank Atkinson

Adrian Babbidge

Stella Bellem

Big Pit Mining Museum, Blaenafon

Stephen Bird

Birmingham City Council, Leisure Services Committee

Hilary Blume

John Blundell

Dr Patrick Boylan

City of Bradford Metropolitan Council

British Association of Friends of Museums

Martin Brown

University of Cambridge, Joint Museums Committee

Cambridgeshire County Museums Advisory Committee

Cambridgeshire Curators Panel

Helen Carpenter

J. E. Chamberlain-Mole

Francis Cheetham

Chelmsford Borough Council

Captain G. W. Clark

David T-D Clarke

Pat Clegg

David E Coke

Dr E. J. T. Collins

Elizabeth Conran

Convention of Scottish Local Authorities

CoRAA Crafts Group

CoRAA Visual Arts Group

Council of Museums in Wales

Stewart Coulter

Alaistair Crawford

Stuart Davies

Colin Dawes

Peter Donnelly

Stephen Douglass

David Downe

Ian Doyle

Martin Drury

Caroline Dudley

East Midlands Museum Service

Ettrick & Lauderdale District Council

Katherine Eustace

Dennis Farr

Dr Margaret L Faull

Dr David Fleming

Tony Ford

Richard Foster

R. J. Fothergill

Alan Gailey

Gateshead Metropolitan Borough Council

Oliver Green

Dr Patrick Greene

Elizabeth Goodhall

Richard J Gornall

Group of Directors of Museums

Dr Jennifer Harris

Dr C Hawe-Smith

Dr John Hayes

Max Hebditch
Mike Hill
Tony Hirst
R. M. Hobby
Denys Hodson

Professor Michael Jaffé
Dr Christine Johnson
Dr Schuyler Jones

Stephen Kay
Professor Martin Kemp
Richard Kilburn

Rowena Lawrence
Local Authority Museums in North
East London Group
Stephen Locke
London Museums Consultative
Committee

Maldon Museum Association
Richard Marks
Colin McLean
Barry Mead
Louise Millard
Dr John Milner
G. B. Morris
Sara Muldoon
The Museums Association
Museums North
Museum Professionals Group

London Borough of Newham,
Leisure Services Committee and
Governing Body of Passmore
Edwards Museum
Newport Borough Council
North of England Museums Service
North West Museum Service
North Western Federation of
Museums & Art Galleries
North Yorkshire County Council

Mark O'Neill
Oxfordshire Museums Advisory
Council

Crispin Paine
David Patmore
Perth and Kinross District Council
Phil Philo
R. L. Pybus
H. V. Radcliffe
Ian Robertson
John Ruffle
Scottish Development Agency
Scottish Education Department
Scottish Museums Council
Scottish Museums Federation
Scottish Tourist Board
Nicholas Serota
Vicky Slowe
Stuart Smith
Society of County Museum
Directors
Society of Local Authority Chief
Executives
Julian Spalding
Standing Committee for Museum
Services in Hertfordshire
Moira Stevenson
Suffolk County Council
Terence Suthers
Kate Thaxton
Michael Thomas
Colin Thompson
John Thompson
Tony Travers
Peter Vigurs
B. E. Vyner
Wales Tourist Board
Alan Warhurst
Giles Waterfield
Welsh Federation of Museums
West Sussex Museums Council
Dr Christopher White
Frank Willett
Barbara Woroncow
Yorkshire and Humberside
Federation of Museums and Art
Galleries
Yorkshire and Humberside
Museums Council

Appendix I *Museums visited*

Big Pit Mining Museum, Blaenafon
City Museum and Art Gallery, Stoke on Trent
Gladstone Pottery Museum, Stoke on Trent
Kelvingrove Art Gallery and Museum, Glasgow
Macclesfield Silk Museum and Heritage Centre
Springburn Museum, Glasgow
Summerlee Heritage Trust, Coatbridge
Tredegar House, Newport
Welsh Folk Museum, St Fagans

Printed in the United Kingdom for HMSO.
Dd.292027, 4/91, C15, 3385/4, 5673, 143626.